Raven Chronicles

Journal, Vol. 24

HOME

Raven Chronicles
Journal, Vol. 24

HOME

Editors

Kathleen Alcalá

Anna Bálint

Phoebe Bosché

Paul Hunter

Stephanie Lawyer

Raven Chronicles Press
Seattle, Washington

FIRST EDITION

ISBN 978-0-9979468-2-6
Library of Congress Control Number: 2017939739

Cover Art: "The Fireplace in the Violinists' House," oil on canvas painting, 35 x 48, 2017, by Rebecca Pye.

Book Design: Phoebe Bosché, using 11/14 Palatino typeface.
Cover Design: Tonya Namura, using Gill Sans typeface.

Established in 1991, *The Raven Chronicles* is a Seattle-based literary organization that publishes and promotes artistic work that embodies the cultural diversity and multitude of viewpoints of writers and artists living in the Pacific Northwest, other regions of the United States, and abroad.

Raven Chronicles Press
Jack Straw Cultural Center
909 NE 43rd Street, Suite 205,
Seattle, Washington 98105-6020

editors@ravenchronicles.org

http://ravenchronicles.org

Remember, Hippopotamus,
as you go upstream
your home
is at the mouth of the river.

—African Proverb

morning walk

Frank Rossini

just beyond the memory
bench where the owl-
eyed man sometimes stops
to stretch & limber where the trail curves
& edges the road   two
vultures spread
their wings & rise into a shiver
of cottonwoods above
a graveled creek

a young buck lies in a patch of spent
camas petals scattered ribs picked
clean his newly antlered head
& hind quarters are still
intact   I hesitate
then move on   vultures patient
creek chanting
young buck dreaming
his way home

TABLE OF CONTENTS

VI Poetics

VII Spoken Word: Stories We Tell

VIII Featured theme: HOME

that's me, dip pen & India ink on paper, by Clare Johnson

Preface

For Raven's Vol. 24 issue, we chose the theme of HOME. We asked writers and visual artists to think about and address the following: The world is in the midst of the largest migration of people since World War II. Due to war and political oppression, many of them will never return to their homelands. Others, like Native Americans in the Americas, have watched as wave after wave of newcomers have come into their land and claimed it as their own. The United States attracts people from all over the world to use as labor, but then denies them a legal opportunity to establish homes and raise families.

Is home a place or a dream of sanctuary? A tarp, bedroll or car parked on the side of the freeway? A ranch you inherited? People you love? A state of mind? An elusive definition of space or location that only the privileged can afford to claim? Describe your home (whatever and wherever it may be) and the things that make it home for you.

In Aleppo, "Abu Hussein, a man in his 50s, was remarkably cheerful as he stood with his wife Umm Hussein and looked down from their balcony on to the rubble that makes his street impassable for any vehicle. 'Nothing is better or more beautiful than our home,' he said. 'It's the place to be in good times or in bad.'"

Here is what our editors have to say about editing this particular issue/theme:

Kathleen Alcalá (fiction editor):

Robert Frost wrote that Home is the place where, when you have to go there, / They have to take you in. That doesn't sound very warm and fuzzy. In reading the submissions so far, there is a strong pull in two directions: the anxiety of having to go there and them having to take you in, and nostalgia for an idealized past or childhood.

The world is changing so quickly that, when people look at the past, at places they once called home, they realize those places can never exist again. We are moving into a time when little is controllable or even predictable. Yet people continue to form families and construct homes with what, and who, we have. Octavia Butler looked into the future with her crystal eye and saw how we would take the rubble of the old and build the new out of it.

Perhaps home is the one place we feel safe. Some people will never have homes, in that case, while others cannot imagine life without it. The remarkable trait of humans is the ability to adapt to extreme circumstances and find home. Perhaps that is what keeps us at the top of the evolutionary heap right now—not our superior abilities, but our adaptability. I still want to hope that the open heart, the compassionate one, will be met with equal compassion. That we can continue to recognize the god in each other, and continue to form homes.

Anna Bálint (Safe Place Writing Circle):

For most people who come to Safe Place Writing Circle the need, longing, and search for home is an intrinsic part of their recovery journey. Home may be a loaded word, connected to homelessness, and nights spent in shelters, in cars, or under bridges; or childhoods spent in foster homes and institutions. In adult life, the word home may have attached itself to broken marriages, or the loss of birth family connections and support due to addiction or mental illness. There may be memories of long stays in hospital, or a history of uprooting and moving on to try someplace new. But home in relation to recovery has other meanings too, such as the relief and comfort of finding affordable housing, a safe environment, a place to unpack and belong. It may mean the contentment that comes with learning to be at home, and at peace, with oneself. And tucked in between the hard times and past traumas, are those good memories of old neighborhoods, or a certain street; of places and times that were home.

Phoebe Bosché (managing editor):

I keep a mental map of North America handy, and try to imagine what each place address of every chosen contributor looks like on that map: sixty-eight writers and fourteen artists / illustrators. The U.S. contributors in this HOME-themed issue live in twenty-one states (Washington, Nebraska, Pennsylvania, California, Vermont, Michigan, Oregon, Illinois, New Jersey, Kansas, Arkansas, Kentucky, Connecticut, Virginia, Utah, Idaho, North Carolina, Massachusetts, New York, North Dakota, Wisconsin); 56% are from Washington State. Several also hail from India, Nigeria, and Canada.

Some artists envisioned home as making sour cherry soup in a kitchen in Budapest; a chimney rising from a fallen-down riverside home; photos of streets from neighborhoods remembered only in longing or that have fallen into despair and desolation; shadows playing on chairs or teacups stacked on a sideboard. Our cover artist, Rebecca Pyle, recreates a fireplace in the home where violin students, including her son, receive lessons, a fireplace "drawn from a memory of a real fireplace . . . *A fireplace is an altar*, said Frank Lloyd Wright . . . and this fireplace is one."

Some contributors envision the idea of home as: "A language structure that is *place* with its multiple meanings of places within place." (Diane Glancy); "The place where I truly feel at home is in a book. This is where the real panoramas are. The landscapes of the human imagination. Oceans, raging rivers, philosophies, forests." (John Olson); "After all, home changes, but stories—be they the stories of former occupants or the stories of travelers visiting a darkened chimney—live forever." (Nyri A. Bakkalian). Inye Wokoma, journalist and filmmaker, created a collage of recollections and meditations about life for a black family in the Central District in Seattle, decades ago; for him home is "about who we imagine ourselves to be and who we aspire to be."

Perhaps the proverb "Your home will always be the place for which you feel the deepest affection, no matter where you are," says it best. Home is where the heart is.

Paul Hunter (poetry editor):

The idea of offering a theme for a magazine issue is to help writers see their work anew in a social context, see it in relation to the needs and concerns of the moment, and maybe help it resonate and connect. A few poets and prose writers reject the idea of a theme altogether. Yet we read their work anyhow, and try to find ways to include them. We all know there are these preoccupations and obsessions we live through, these memes that seize the group mind and for a while are everywhere we turn, local memes, regional and national memes, and ones that reach beyond, to the common human spirit. So thank you for joining in the game, the dance, sharing what you make of your own thoughts and images of home, the elusive felt life that is forever home and far from here.

Stephanie Lawyer (nonfiction editor):

The nonfiction submissions for this issue are most striking because of their across-the-board interpretations of what home means. Home is a physical space that provides shelter and security, and with that can come familiarity and ease. Then again, it can be a state of mind. As John Olson writes, "Home is quintessentially a feeling": the pleasure of discovering new landscapes through books, or the comfort of coming home to a relationship after revisiting the past, or the release of shedding your skin and starting over again somewhere new. And, in counterpoint, there are also reactions to loss of home: mournfulness in the face of a community unraveling, disorientation when assimilation tears at the fabric of a native language, outrage at being prevented from claiming both identity and home as your own.

In the light of world events that have left millions uprooted, this mix of perspectives on home makes complete sense. So does the common thread running through these essays: a longing for empathy and reciprocity.

I

Bridges Not Walls

Bridge Over Center, photo by David Anderson

Women's March #1, photo by Anna Bálint

The Fempire Strikes Back

Anna Bálint

A woman's place is in the resistance
My existence is resistance

I will not go quietly back into the 1950s
Empathy not bigotry
Abort misogyny
Keep your rosaries off my ovaries
Same shit, different century

Hate does not make America great
Love louder than they can hate
Making America sick again?
Make America Think Again

Don't mess with Mother Earth
This is your Mother speaking
Respect your Mother
Stand with Standing Rock
Water is life
Science is real

A woman's place is in the resistance
My existence is resistance

The future is nasty
I am a nasty woman
Je suis nasty women
Nasty women keep fighting
Nasty as we wanna be

We the resilient
We are the medicine
We will not take one step backwards
We won't give up, we wont give in
We can do it. We are not things
We are all Wonderwoman

White silence equals violence
Black Lives Matter
Muslim Lives Matter
White silence is white violence
I'll see you nice white ladies
at the next Black Lives Matter march
. . . right?

This feminist has balls
Bridges not walls
I didn't come out of the closet for this shit
I'm here, I'm queer, I refuse to live in fear
Tiny hands can't hold back progress
Tiny hands off my rights
Can't build a wall, hands too small
Men of quality don't fear equality
Nasty women = bad hombres

A woman's place is in the resistance
My existence is resistance

My pussy, my rules
This pussy grabs back
Keep your policy out of my pussy
Ne touche pas my pussy
Pussies against patriarchy
Viva la Vulva!

Let us not grow weary
Love across enemy lines
Love, rise, resist
Resist, revolt, repeat
Stand up, speak up, show up
Unbought, unbossed.
Rise up! And still we rise

A woman's place is in the resistance
My existence is resistance
Shout with outrage, sing with hope
The Fempire Strikes back!

On January 21, 2017, the Women's March brought millions of people into the streets across this country and around the globe. I was one of them. Marching in Seattle, the city's hills afforded an opportunity to take in the vast, and seemingly endless human river both in front of and behind me as it swept down Jackson Street and into the downtown corridor. And riding along on that river were bobbing signs and banners of all shapes and sizes and colors that gave expression to the mind-boggling and inspiring diversity, scope, inclusiveness, and creativity that characterized the Women's March. Those signs were the impetus for this "found" poem, every line of which I borrowed from a sign.

The Wall

Anita Endrezze

Build a wall of saguaros,
butterflies, and bones
of those who perished
in the desert. A wall of worn shoes,
dry water bottles, poinsettias.
Construct it of gilded or crazy house
mirrors so some can see their true faces.
Build a wall of revolving doors
or revolutionary abuelas.
Make it as high as the sun, strong as tequila.
Boulders of sugar skulls. Adobe or ghosts.
A Lego wall or bubble wrap. A wall of hands
holding hands, hair braided from one woman
to another, one country to another.
A wall made of Berlin. A wall made for tunneling.
A beautiful wall of taco trucks.
A wall of silent stars and migratory songs.
This wall of solar panels and holy light,
panels of compressed cheetos,
topped not by barbed wire but sprouting
avocado seeds, those Aztec testicles.
A wall to keep Us in and Them out.
It will have faces and heartbeats.
Dreams will be terrorists. The Wall will divide
towns, homes, mountains,
the sky that airplanes fly through
with their potential illegals.
Our wallets will be on life support
to pay for it. Let it be built
of guacamole so we can have a bigly block party.
Mortar it with xocoatl, chocolate. Build it from coyote howls
and wild horses drumming across the plains of Texas,

from the memories
of hummingbird warriors and healers.
Stack it thick as blood, which has mingled
for centuries, la vida. Dig the foundation deep.
Create a 2,000 mile altar, lit with votive candles
for those who have crossed over
defending freedom under spangled stars
and drape it with rebozos,
and sweet grass.
Make it from two-way windows:
the wind will interrogate us,
the rivers will judge us, for they know how to separate
and divide to become whole.
Pink Floyd will inaugurate it.
Ex-Presidente Fox will give it the middle finger salute.
Wiley Coyote will run headlong into it,
and survive long after history forgets us.
Bees will find sand-scoured holes and fill it
with honey. Heroin will cover it in blood.
But it will be a beautiful wall. A huge wall.
Remember to put a rose-strewn doorway in Nogales
where my grandmother crossed over,
pistols on her hips. Make it a gallery of graffiti art,
a refuge for tumbleweeds,
a border of stories we already know by heart.

Walls and Bridges

Maiah Merino

Growing up in Compton, California, the part of Compton where even people from there didn't want to go—we had walls at every corner. Although some would say imaginary, territory was territory. When you crossed into another gang's territory without permission, there were consequences. We had alliances with another gang because of my brother, so we could travel quite a ways without being bothered by anyone. And by we, I mean my younger brother and I. On most days we walked all the way to the pool around the corner, past the farmer's market, five blocks from our house, across the street from the statue of La Virgen and our Catholic school, Our Lady of the Rosary, and not get stopped. But on our way back, often someone would stand in front of us on the sidewalk, block our passage until we told them my brother's name and we were let by, unharmed. I acted like I didn't care, I wasn't afraid, when I knew they could knife or kill us at any second. We walked our streets not seeing anything, like the drug deals going down, or people being robbed or harassed, because if they caught us looking, we were next. We all knew the rules. And even with the enforced police curfews, you could still hear gunshots in my neighborhood at night.

Those walls: mine and theirs made sense.

My mom also had a wall around her rose garden, one of those cement ones, to keep the roses from getting trampled on by my three brothers—"desgraciados, que no puedan a dejar nada en paz y no respetan ningún persona"—she spit as she yelled at them. Each rose represented one of us and our birth months, so she talked to them like they were us. "Your younger brother's Amarillo está un poco flaco y enfermo, pobrecito: Yellow, skinny and sickly." My younger brother was born two months premature and always seemed needy, like he was lacking something. He got teased a lot in our family. "Yours is doing okay," she would say, "un poco henosa como ti a veces se ve anaranjado y otros dias morado como si no puede decidir quien era: moody like you." Some days it looks orange and other days purple, like it can't even decide who it wants to be. My two older brothers: machismo flowers. Bright crimson, pert. Vibrantly puffed, but tended to get bugs that infested the rest of us. She talked of transplanting them into a separate garden.

Mom was most enchanted with her own mango-watermelon variety, "mira como se sientan anciosas y nerviosas." She was obsessed with how anxious and worried they always looked. She talked to them about their spots and told them they would be okay. She fed them coffee grounds from her morning café, which was ceremonial for her; she said it made their soil stronger and gave them extra nutrients.

When I got older, left LA to go to a private, predominantly white, wealthy college, I learned about bridges. There were no bridges anywhere I travelled in LA, so I had never physically travelled across one before moving to the Northwest. I loved them at first sight: the way they connected land over water. Their complex architecture. And like seeing trees I had never seen before, outside of palm or orange, bridges were passages into new territory.

I was the first of my siblings to finish high school and go to college, on both sides of the family: my brothers and I didn't think we would live to be eighteen. So when I felt dirty, unknown, and alien because I was surrounded by a bunch of white people who had never been around a brown person, I dreamt about Nana's tortillas. Gorditas, she called them. They were smaller and chunkier than most, with her chuckle of laughter teasing the masa as she patted and shaped them. Nana's gorditas. Anyone would get out of bed for those, water the garden, clean the bathroom, whatever she asked if she would just make them for us. And she took advantage of this, waiting until enough of us were up, to hand out her list of chores as she began making the masa. It really doesn't take long to mix and make tortillas, but, like I said, her laughter, watching us waiting for her and doing our chores that had to be completed before she would finish, was good Catholic torture.

I missed how everything made sense there, and the smell of good, home-cooked Mexican food. I met some Latinos from small towns in Washington and we tried to turn college food dishes into something edible, but it was the challenge—like each meal was a research experiment that needed to solved—that kept us motivated. They often brought back from home tortillas, tamales, arroz or frijoles to cheer me up. There weren't many of us, so we sheltered one another.

In my junior year I took a class called the *Ethics of Non-Violence* and read books by Martin Luther King, Gandhi, Dorothy Day, and Thich Nhat Hahn—I felt challenged, understood and in conflict. These leaders passionately loved their families, cultures, and causes, and showed this by their non-violence. I wanted to be like them, yet conflict, in and of itself, to me meant: war, gangs, weapons, rage, anger, paybacks. I could see that these writers and their belief systems represented me more than my childhood environment because, although I was surrounded by and raised amongst violence, I did not become violent. I did not believe that way. And now, I could see there could be another way. I realized I could never go back. I could never go back. Born and raised in silence and secrets, where language was felt, smelled, or seen by that look in the eye that told you whether someone was with you or not: that was shattered.

It was then I became a writer.

Well, I had actually begun writing when I was in sixth grade, journaling our lives, and writing poetry that seemed like a whole bunch of feelings floating around words on a page. Yet, somehow in college, in a place so different from where I was raised, the stories awoke in me. And redemption was a major theme. I was obsessed with figuring out how to make up for the sins of my brothers. So, we are back to the roses. My brother's roses were transplanted. My mom decided she couldn't handle having to suffer for their regular bug infestations, so she sent my brothers away, or they ran away. Life was both better and scarier when they were gone. With them gone, those bushes, their flower bushes, infected and infested one another. And this was also true in life.

Transplanted, I, too, flourished in new soil and began to understand the importance of leaving behind a polluted land, to begin developing a mind influenced by both my life as lived, and the possibility of something entirely new.

II

Words From the Café

48th Street, photo by David Anderson

The Recovery Café

An Introduction

The Recovery Café sits on the corner of Boren and Denny, in downtown Seattle. It is a unique and remarkable place. "Recovery Café and its School for Recovery serve men and women who have suffered trauma, homelessness, addiction and / or other mental health challenges. In this loving community, men and women experience belonging, healing and the joy of contributing. The Café and School for Recovery help participants develop tools for maintaining recovery and stabilizing in mental / physical health, housing, relationships and employment / volunteer service." —*Excerpt from mission statement, Recovery Café website.*

Writer / teacher, Anna Bálint, joined the Café community as a volunteer, teaching writing classes with the School of Recovery. Over time, her classes evolved into "Safe Place Writing Circle," an ongoing and fluid group that has met weekly since Fall, 2012. Its purpose is to provide a "safe place" for Café members to creatively explore many different aspects of their lives through writing, give voice to their beliefs, hopes and fears, and discover the power of their own voices. Some amazing stories and poems emerge, on a regular basis, from everyone involved. Here are a few of those voices.

Home

Megan McInnis

Home is where my mother is. I've never said that before, but now that she's dead I feel very strongly that, if she were alive somewhere, that would be home.

Today is my mother's birthday. She would have been seventy-five. She'd been painfully ill for a year, but only in her last two months did we know her illness would be fatal. Vasculitis is a disease that kills arteries and destroys tissues, and she had ulcers on both ankles—one of them going all the way down to the bone. They caused her to scream in agony, and having her bandages changed twice a week made her cry.

But one of the worst parts of my mom's illness was the dementia, which worsened over the months. Toward the end, she was often crazy; one day she said, "This doesn't look like my house. I want to go home." She ran through all the rooms, shrugging off my stepdad and her caregiver, Annette, who were finally able to stop her from running downstairs and out the front door. Over the next few days she referred to that episode as the time Annette tried to throw her down the stairs—when really Annette had been pushing her *up* the stairs.

It's awful when someone you love is crazy—especially when the craziness causes her anguish. How could we convince her she *was* home? She didn't feel right. Bob gave her some Haldol, an antipsychotic, and that calmed her down.

You can't feel at home physically if you don't feel at home in your mind. I told my mother (though who knows how much she understood) that I take an antipsychotic, too—Zyprexa—which, together with Prozac, reduces my bipolar disorder. I wanted her to know she wasn't the only lunatic.

With my medications, I'm starting to feel more at home

in my mind. But I miss my mom. A wonderful woman at my church, who I've known more than forty years, sent me a card yesterday saying that she knew I must want to have my mom here with me on her birthday. Ethel was right; I want her here so much.

But I've been trying to make a new home for myself. Christopher and I are back together—wonderfully, happily back together—and, this time around, he pays for all his own food and part of the rent. Since he can't afford a full half of the rent, he does all the cooking and cleaning—*all* of it—and, best of all, brings my coffee to me in the morning. He also keeps his belongings tidily packed away in the storage closet on my deck, so that the house still feels like my own. And I've made an altar with my mother's picture that I go to every day, lighting a candle, bowing my head all the way to the floor, and saying a prayer to my mother.

Making sour cherry soup, Anna's kitchen, Budapest, 2013, photo by Anna Bálint

Harlem

Johnnie Powell

125th Street, Harlem. Walking up and down this street was like popcorn popping. Everywhere I looked something alive was taking place. The famous Apollo Theater, where the great entertainers came from all over the country to make us feel good. Where I first heard the Temptations sing and Richard Pryor tell filthy jokes. Where I saw the first Ali-Frazier fight. Earlier, I'd I heard Malcolm X stand in front of the Apollo and talk about the condition of African Americans in America, where he would grab the broom of anger and drive off the beast of fear. Where Nikki read her poetry about love, and made your soul crawl out from its hiding place.

Everywhere you went, from the East Side to the West Side, music was playing. People were dancing in the streets, playing cards, shooting dice, selling clothes, selling books. Discussion everywhere about Dear Lord. About democracy, and where do I appear in it? And churches everywhere. Finding religion was like finding the right pair of shoes. Finding the one that fit you. And don't let anybody make you wear the wrong shoes. Harlem, and the faces of the people, my people. Where the strongest hearts have the most scars, where lambs became lions. Home.

I went home to 125th Street, New York, about four years ago and all that has changed. Now Harlem is a yuppie haven. Bill Clinton has an office on this street. Where I once never saw a white person, now I don't see any black people. Harlem has changed. But I don't let yesterday take up too much of today. Like riding the iron horse—the subway leaving uptown: it used to cost $.50, now it's $3.00. Life is not about chance, life is about change!

At Home With MySelf and I

Cathy Scott

I'm home, and so happy am I to see MySelf is also home. I will pour MySelf a cup of wine and spread a bit of cheese on our favorite crackers. Perhaps someone else might look down on Ritz crackers and frown at their presence beside the cheap box of wine: cheap only for those who can afford more refined grapes. MySelf and I are quite content with boxed wine and Ritz crackers spread lavishly with Philly Cream Cheese. Only the best for the poorest us. And I fancy that we enjoy it much more than snobs with more "refined" palates.

Our recliner welcomes MySelf and I. We relax and converse easily. We have, after all, known each other for sixty-six years, so the oldest and dearest of friends are we. When no one else is around and, sometimes, even when they are, MySelf and I have our little talks and jokes and secrets. We both sigh in grief grown lighter when shared. The loss of husband and soulmate, and all the dear family and friends who departed and left us. MySelf and I vow never to leave each other. Not ever!

We lean back and turn on the TV. MySelf and I both love the same programs, hate the same commercials. We both sip wine and enjoy the special treat the crackers provide. We both agree that at our age calories are our enemy, and our waistline reminds us daily.

Yep, at home with Myself and I, and our younger selves, plus three cats. A family grown by one new kitty headed for the shelter recently rescued by My Self and I. This is My life / Our life, and one to be envied if only everyone knew just how contented we are, and just how much love is shared in this joined heart. Yep, at home with Myself and I . . . and occasionally Me drops by to join us.

Home is Where the Heart is Safe

Jay Scott

If I woke up this morning to four walls and a roof,
could I or would I call it home?

A home should be: A safe place. A sanctuary.
A temple. A place for comfort. A safe place to feel pain.
A place for healing, for resting, rejuvenating.
A place of nourishment. A place to grow.

Home is where the heart is safe.

But life is a tricky thing, full of ups and downs
and all arounds. Home is a pyramid.
A structure made of blocks.
Blocks built into walls, four walls and a roof.

1 Safety
2 Comfort
3 Rest
4 Rejuvenation
5 Nourishment
6 Growth

But if life starts to take away, say 1&5 6&4 3&2
then I'm left in ruin.
Still my heart beats, and life goes on . . .

Mountains and plains, a rectangle state. Columbine flowers.
Dry hot summers and snow-filled winters. Wilderness, trees,
lots to see and to do. Camping, exploring. City full of
Nuggets and Broncos. Avalanche and Rockies.

It was once home . . . until I lost . . . 1&4 6&2 3&5
Ashes to ashes, my heart keeps beating.

Gateway to the west. Another day, another dollar.
First car. First home. First child.
A high school diploma and teenage dreams full of ice cream
and wedding cakes. A sea of cardinals, red and white.

Living my casino dream, until I lost . . . 5&4 1&2 3&6
My heart keeps beating.

Nine months of rain, a happy start.
The Pacific Northwest. Rain and bark. Casinos and Kids.
New Apartment. New car. Much life to live.

But time is ironic.
I move through time and lose my 1&2 3&4 5&6
My heart keeps beating . . .
but this time I'm left with nothing . . .

Silence.

Thump thump, thump thump.
Thump thump, thump thump.
Thump thump, thump thump.

I am still here, my heart still beats
and I choose to live and adapt.
I am homeless but never alone,
my heart still beating wherever I call home.

Home

Susan Tekola

Home, I was told,
was mother's womb holding a brown baby
created from two people who hated each other.
Still, a child was born, into an unsafe world
and layers of generational trauma.

Home. It never was my refuge.
Foster home, group homes that were really
not homes at all: Governmental systems.
Shall I call those home? That's why I broke away.

Discovered a new shelter behind locked doors,
loss of the ability to feel, no longer a need to hide
It was supposed to keep me safe;
there was no freedom, but that's okay . . . right?

Discharged and reunited with my people
and their wounds; family for me.
Trying to change, trying to heal, not to repeat
the broken child that was me.

I learned to keep on walking,
and run if I had to hide. To bury the parts
that made me cry for far too long.
Do not judge. Do not fight.

It took me right back into a place called home.
This time it is home, a home that I get to make,
that this time I will rebuild with Faith
and Hope, Recovery, and Healing.
Shall we be? Shall we begin to smile and love
at home?

III

The Family Corvidae

Raven, photo by Bill Yake

Possession

T. Clear

From a web of dreamless sleep
I wake before dawn
to an alarm of crows,

open the door
to their frantic swerving
top of the pine

where a lone eagle
clutches the highest branch,
unnerved by attack.

I doubt an eagle cares
about ownership of a tree,
but nineteen years of possession

of a house beneath these boughs
has convinced me the crows own the pine
outright, no back payments,

no outstanding debt to nature.
No court will remand it, nor judgment
tear it from their claws.

Not even the eagle, who eventually
lifts his wings in a sauntering swoop,
disappears into the grey veil.

Pre-school Logic

Larry Eickstaedt

It took considerable coaxing
with peanuts before one brave crow
came to accept my offerings.

Unlike the bird,
she was not at all hesitant
to come up to the porch.

As her mommy gardened next door,
little Vera marched up on the porch
demanding to know
"Where is your elephant?"

After whispering that
I had no elephant,
she adamantly replied,
"Well, I was here yesterday
and saw the peanuts!"

from **Clownery**

Paul Hunter

THE MOMENT WAS DREAMLIKE, UPSETTING. The clown was under the back end of the car on a sunny afternoon, bleeding the brakes while his nephew pumped and held the pedal. Out of nowhere a thump hit the car. He heard his nephew say What the hell. He crawled out from under and stood up. There was a dead crow at his feet, still warm, not breathing, not a mark on it, nothing ruffled or broke. Four other crows perched in the trees all around, hollering bloody murder. Do something, they seemed to shout. But what was there to do? He got a shovel and buried the crow in the garden while they watched. It seemed glossy and perfect, neither male nor female, neither old nor young. He laid it in the hole with the blade of the shovel, then sprinkled in a little dirt, that couldn't help but look wrong. There was no service, from the assembled mourners not a sound. Then his nephew said, The crow just tumbled down from the sky, out of the middle of its life.

IV

Food & Culture

Budapest Windowsill, 2013, photo by Anna Bálint

Letter of Thanks for a One-Ingredient Cereal

Mark Trechock

Dear friends in Beloit, Wisconsin, my thanks
and my congratulations for placing Alf's cereal,
whose only ingredient is hard red spring wheat,
here at the big box store in our little town,
which oil's big boom has turned into
a mixing bowl for the world, and stirred
together our human ingredients.

The stockers in the cheese-and-lunch-meat aisle
speak what sounds like west African French,
while a Mexican rig hand peers down
the long highway of shelves, searching
for landmarks of home, like the queso fresco,
which contains only milk and enzymes.
Pillow-sized bags of dried pasilla peppers,
which admit not a single other substance,
already lie in his shopping cart, full
of the heartwarming taste of home
that gives a muchacho the cojones
to carry on in the midst of chaos.

Down the cereal aisle, however,
yours is the sole exception
to all the shelved cereal boxes,
whose multi-syllabic, incomprehensible,
fine-print show-off lists of ingredients
only ancient Greek manuscript scholars
or corporate plant breeders may hope to decipher,
and which (despite all their plain English
braggadocio in 40-pica red print on the front,

about newness and flavor and fun)
taste only of sugar and something
swept up from the floor with a broom.

Standing in line for the cash register
with plenty of time to ponder my surroundings,
I watch an elderly woman signing a check as if
she expected a discount for good penmanship,
a family leaning on three shopping carts (containing
eleven loaves of plastic-wrapped white bread),
and a roughneck with at least two dozen
one-serving microwave dishes with lots of cheese.

At the till, I exchange pidgin pleasantries
with a cashier from somewhere in the Middle East,
in whose placid smile I read disassociation,
or perhaps a strong longing to speak
without first having to translate in her head.

Once out the door I plan to drive north on the highway,
then head east somewhere just past the Green River,
which trickles off in the general direction of Beloit,
to look at the hard red spring wheat stalks,
which rise within two miles of the grocery aisles
and make their way up from the mysterious
underground nutrients toward the lingering late June dusk,
leaning to the northwest in a light breeze,
which to the trained prairie nose suggests
a good rain sometime later in the week.

V

Odes to Persons, Places & Things

Back East, photo by David Anderson

Streets of Chicago, photo by Gabe Hales

Xicago, March, 2015

Jim Cantú

Mounting stairs to train in Xicago's Pilsen, nuestro barrio.
Magnificent mural stares me square in the face,
Two civilizations struggle for dominance.
Knights, Mixteca Eagle, and Spanish Conquistador,
Locked in death's embrace.
Blood mingles, and so do our cultures,
lines blurred as vanquished hides traditions in that of victor.

And what is vanquished, when does the victor win?
Is it that last major battle? The last city lost?
Is it the campaign of Terror,
where native mothers are hung from trees,
with their children hung from their ankles?

Does a struggle continue, past the memory of one generation,
to the legacy of 10 generations, 20 generations?
Nahautl and other indigenous languages are still spoken in
  our mountain villages.
The 2500-year-old Mayan calendar still used for planting in
  Guatemala and elsewhere in our lands.
Those in power still seek to destroy dissent,
Like the 43 lives stolen from Collegio Ayotzinapa,
  Iguala, Guererro.
The struggle does not end,
We remember.

I had just left the National Museum of Mexican Art in Chicago's Pilsen neighborhood, which is predominantly Mexican-American. The L Station was filled with amazing artwork. As I mounted the stairs to the train's elevated platform I saw a mural of two figures locked in death's struggle. This poem was inspired by that mural.

VI

Poetics

Seeing Shapes, photo by Gabe Hales

Even in Seattle:
An Introduction to Haiku Poetry

Michael Dylan Welch

Haiku are short poems from Japan that celebrate the seasons. They are now written around the world in many languages, even in Seattle, and you can write them too. The following are four haiku poems, one for each season of the year:

the crane's legs
a little shorter—
spring rain

short night—
beads of dew
on the furry caterpillar

grave visiting—
my old dog
leads the way

a soft rustling
through the bamboo—
nighttime snow

These poems are by the four great haiku masters of Japan: Bashō, Buson, Issa, and Shiki. Can you see how the crane's legs look shorter to Bashō because of a fresh spring rain? On a hot summer night, are you as sleepless as Buson who notices a caterpillar at dawn? Like Issa, do you feel even older than your beloved dog who knows the way to a grave you traditionally visit in the autumn? And do you, like Shiki, delight in the magical sound of gently falling snow? Can you feel what these poets felt? Do these poems put you there by the water, in the garden, in town, or in the country? If you take a moment to dwell in each poem, you will experience what the poet experienced, and feel what the poet felt.

This is the aim of haiku, to help you know the world around you a little better, through your five senses, to intuitively grasp the essence of what it means to be alive. In a *Paris Review* interview in 2001, Billy Collins says that haiku demonstrates "existential gratitude," adding that "Almost every haiku says the same thing: 'It's amazing to be alive here.'" A good haiku lets you feel simple yet profound emotions about ordinary life, and helps you be more deeply aware of nature's unfolding pageant of seasons. These short poems show you the uncommon in the common, the extraordinary in the ordinary, helping you to notice what is too easily unnoticed. As translator R. H. Blyth once wrote, "Haiku shows us what we knew all the time, but did not know we knew; it shows us that we are poets in so far as we live at all."

Here are two famous haiku in Japanese and English, first by Bashō, and then by Buson:

古池や蛙飛こむ水の音　　芭蕉

furuike ya
kawazu tobikomu
mizu no oto

old pond—
a frog jumps in
water's sound

身にしむやなき妻のくしを閨に踏　　蕪村

mi ni shimu ya
naki tsuma no kushi wo
neya ni fumu

a piercing chill—
I step on my dead wife's comb
in our bedroom

Haiku poetry is one of Japan's best-known art forms, and is now written around the world. To make a haiku succeed, the poet carefully describes an image or experience to create an emotion or insight in the reader. This realization is often referred to as an "aha" moment that some people think of as a taste of enlightenment. A leap of some kind exists in each haiku, and it's up to you, as the reader, to find it, often in the jump from one of the poem's two parts to the other.

Traditional haiku uses concrete images to convey an experience or sensory perception typically taking place in one of the four seasons. Japanese haiku evoke the seasons by using a *kigo* or season word, such as "frog" for spring or "snow" for winter. Haiku also employ a *kireji* or cutting word to divide the poem into two juxtaposed parts. Japanese haiku are written in a single vertical line, and typically follow a pattern of 5-7-5 sounds, which are not the same as English syllables. Many people think a haiku is simply any words arranged in three lines of 5-7-5 syllables, but this is not accurate. This is really a violation of the Japanese form, not a preservation of it. The word "haiku," for example, counts as two syllables, but three sounds in Japanese. Linguists and literary critics have observed that about 10 to 14 English syllables are equivalent to the 17 sounds of a Japanese haiku. In English, literary haiku use three lines to imply natural and human seasonal phenomena. They are frequently objective and imagistic, instead of being subjective, analytical, or judgmental. They usually avoid titles, rhyme, and most overt metaphor and simile. Haiku relies on images perceived through the five senses to convey meaning to the reader in the here and now. Haiku also has a cousin, known as *senryu*, that tends to focus on human nature in a humorous or satirical way rather than focusing on seasonal perceptions.

Here's an empathetic winter haiku by Buson:

tethered horse—
snow
in both stirrups

The Origin of Haiku

Where did haiku come from? The term *haiku,* or "playful verse," is only about a hundred years old, and was coined in the late 1800s by Shiki, one of Japan's great haiku masters. Before then, haiku were known as *hokku,* which means "starting verse." The hokku began a linked verse form known as *renga,* written by two or more poets. In a renga, the first verse (in a pattern of 5-7-5 sounds) was followed by a verse in a 7-7 pattern, followed by another 5-7-5 verse, and so on. Renga were typically written in lengths of 100 verses, sometimes even 1,000. The hokku poem set the tone for the entire renga, yet was also deliberately fragmentary and "incomplete," a trait still evident in haiku today. Readers "finished" the poem in their imaginations. Hokku also commemorated the season in which the renga was written, and this seasonal element is still central to the haiku art. Bashō, the first great master of what became known as haiku, wrote mostly *haikai no renga* in a pattern of 36 verses (the modern term is *renku*), and his hokku were so good that his students collected them separately from the renga where they first appeared. It was not until the 1890s, though, thanks to the efforts of Shiki, that haiku became a truly independent poem. Here's a haiku by Shiki, who was gravely ill with tuberculosis towards the end of his life:

> again and again
> I keep asking
> how high the snow is

Bashō

Of the four great masters who dominated haiku in Japan, the first was Matsuo Bashō, who lived from 1644 to 1694. Bashō came from a samurai family and spent much of his life traveling and writing haikai no renga.

Tea II, photo by Jenn Powers

He also wrote *haibun*, which was a mixture of autobiographical prose with haiku, often in the form of travel diaries. His most famous diary is the *Oku no hosomichi*, or *The Narrow Road to the Interior*. This book was not just about the interior of northern Japan, where he traveled on foot for many months, but was a journey to his psychological and spiritual interior as well. Bashō has been called the "Shakespeare" of Japan, and Japanese schoolchildren memorize Bashō's most famous poems. Bashō once said to "Learn of the pine tree from the pine tree, learn of the bamboo from the bamboo," and this is good advice for anyone wishing to write haiku with depth and empathy.

Here are three poems by Bashō:

a crow settles
on a bare branch—
autumn evening

from cherry trees,
into salads, soups, and everywhere,
blossoms fall

deep autumn—
I wonder how
my neighbour lives

Buson

The second of Japan's four great haiku masters was Yosa Buson. Compared to Bashō, who wrote his poems from a Zen-influenced spiritual perspective, Buson was more humanistic. He lived from 1716 to 1783, and not only excelled at haiku, but at painting as well. In Japan, Buson's paintings are now considered national treasures. One type of painting that he excelled at was *haiga*, which is the art of harmoniously combining haiku, calligraphy, and brush painting. Buson's poems were often strongly objective, employing an immediacy and imagism that we might expect from an accomplished painter. Through literary allusion, Buson helped to revive an appreciation for Bashō's poetry, even while he added his own strong, distinctive, and sometimes philosophical voice to the history of Japanese haiku.

Here are three of Buson's poems:

such coolness—
the bell's sound
leaving the bell

summer river—
I cross it with sandals
here in my hand

sleeping in—
cherry blossoms stuck
to the soles of my shoes

Issa

Kobayashi Issa is often considered the most endearing and lovable of Japan's four great haiku masters. This is because he wrote so appreciatively about small and seemingly insignificant things. His poems about snails, fleas, sparrows, and crickets epitomize his folksy and empathetic style. Issa lived a hard life, from 1763 to 1828, undergoing repeated personal and family tragedies. His mother died when he was three, his stepmother despised him and made him work in the fields instead of going to school, he was forced to leave home at fourteen, and he lived a life of much poverty. Although he later married and found some literary success as a haiku poet, his children died very young, as did one of his wives. Yet he wrote 20,000 mostly joyous haiku in his lifetime, influenced by his practice of Pure Land Buddhism. Indeed, the best of Issa's haiku are remembered for their intimacy, buoyancy, and indomitable joy.

in this world
we walk on the roof of hell
gazing at flowers

Issa's poems are deservedly among the best-loved poems of Japan. Here are three more:

melting snow—
the village flooded
with children

the radish puller
points my way
with a radish

bugs on a branch
floating down the river,
still singing

Shiki

Masaoka Shiki, the fourth of the four great masters of Japanese haiku, lived from 1867 to 1902. He is said to have coined the term *haiku*. This was part of his successful effort to recognize the *hokku* (the starting verse of longer linked verses) as a separate and independent genre of poetry. Shiki was sometimes critical of Bashō, giving more favor to the imagism of Buson, yet, in the process, he helped to revive and elevate haiku. He was also innovative with *tanka* (a longer and much older cousin to haiku, written in a pattern of 5-7-5-7-7 sounds, often about love). In haiku, Shiki emphasized the technique of *shasei*, or "sketching from life." With this technique, he promoted the use of objectivity in haiku, enabling the image to show rather than to tell. Despite the tuberculosis that he suffered from through much of his short life, Shiki probably had more influence than any other poet on modern haiku in Japan and even around the world.

Shiki revolutionized haiku with his commentary and criticism, opening the door to broader variety and experimentation. Many of his own haiku, however, were fairly traditional, and he valued discipline, aesthetics, and careful crafting. Here are three Shiki poems:

rear window—
a woman's face looking out
at the falling snow

my body pressed
against the plaster wall—
such heat

my view of it
through a hole in the shoji—
slanting snow

Chiyo-ni

The poet Chiyo-ni should rightly be considered a "fifth" master of Japanese haiku of equal stature to Bashō, Buson, Issa, and Shiki. That she has not been recognized equally was largely because of patriarchal traditions in Japanese society, but she is easily Japan's most celebrated female haiku poet. Chiyo-ni lived from 1703 to 1775. In her 50s, she became a Buddhist nun to pursue her poetic art, because nuns did not have the normal social expectations imposed on them that other women had. Being a nun gave her the freedom to write. This freedom nurtured Chiyo-ni's heart and helped her to produce her best poems. Chiyo-ni's approach to haiku, like that of Bashō and Issa, was spiritual and compassionate. She often wrote about impermanence, thereby celebrating its sad beauty. Like Buson, Chiyo-ni also excelled at *haiga*, or haiku painting.

Here are three poems by Chiyo-ni, the first of which is about her son who had died:

> I wonder where
> he chases dragonflies today,
> my lost little boy

> the morning glory
> entangles the well bucket—
> I seek water elsewhere

> coming home—
> not a word to say
> after moon viewing

Contemporary Haiku in Japan

Translator R. H. Blyth once wrote that "A haiku is . . . a hand beckoning, a door half-opened, a mirror wiped clean. It is a way of returning to nature, to our moon nature, our cherry blossom nature, our falling leaf nature, in short, to our Buddha nature." He also said, "It is a way in which the cold winter rain, the swallows of evening, even the very day in its hotness, and the length of the night become truly alive, share in our humanity, speak their own silent and expressive language." In Japan, haiku attracts many millions of practitioners. According to the *Kadokawa Haiku Almanac*, in 2006 Japan had 835 known haiku groups, each typically having a monthly meeting known as a *kukai* where members vote anonymously for the best poems submitted by members. Most of these groups publish a journal, typically monthly, and each issue contains many hundreds of haiku. One of Japan's largest haiku journals, *Hototogisu*, is available at newsstands across the country. It has perhaps the longest ongoing lineage—Shiki published in the journal more than a hundred years ago. *Hototogisu* has 15,000 members who receive the publication monthly, and each issue typically has about 350 pages and 10,000 haiku. Japan obviously has a complex and active haiku scene. Television shows regularly feature haiku, including, in English, the current *Haiku Masters* program on NHK, available through Comcast cable television in the Pacific Northwest. In addition, many cities maintain museums for haiku literature and its leading poets. You can find haiku in restaurants and hotels, in temples and shrines, on haiku stones by the side of the road, on soft drink cans sold in vending machines, and in daily newspaper columns read by tens of millions of people every day. Matsuyama, Shiki's birthplace, is often called "Haiku Country" because of the many famous haiku poets who were born there, and you can find nearly a hundred "haiku boxes" all around the city where you can share your poems. In Japan, haiku is not only a highly respected literary vocation but also an adored pastime of ordinary people. The beauty of haiku is how these unassuming poems celebrate the ordinary. Their brevity makes them easy to write, and they are even easier to enjoy, because of the powerful emotions that they evoke through sensory imagery. Everyone can celebrate life through haiku.

Here's a selection of haiku by five contemporary Japanese poets. These translations are by Emiko Miyashita and Michael Dylan Welch:

紅梅の莟は固し言はず　　　　高浜虚子
kōbai no tsubomi wa katashi mono iwazu

the red plum's
flower buds are tight—
I say nothing
—Kyoshi Takahama

秋来ぬと思ふ木蔭に入るたび　鷹羽狩行
aki kinu to omou kokage ni hairu tabi

autumn has come—
or so I think, whenever I enter
a tree's shade
—Shugyō Takaha

夜桜を映せる水の深さかな　有馬朗人
yozakura wo utsuseru mizu no fukasa kana

the depth of water
reflecting cherry blossoms
at night
—Akito Arima

秋澄むと石垣に手を当てにけり　井上弘美
akisumu to ishigaki ni te wo ate ni keri

saying how clear
the autumn is, I touch
a stone fence
—Hiromi Inoue

水槽に橋を沈める立夏かな　宮下恵美子
suisō ni hashi wo shizumeru rikka kana

I sink a little bridge
to the aquarium floor—
first day of summer
—Emiko Miyashita

Contemporary Haiku in English

French philosopher Roland Barthes once wrote that "haiku has this rather fantasmagorical property: that we always suppose we ourselves can write such things easily." Haiku do indeed look easy to write, but to write them well can be much more challenging than the superficial way they are typically taught in schools. As already mentioned, haiku is usually mistaught as being a 5-7-5-syllable poem, yet this is not only inaccurate but neglects requirements of the genre that are more important than form—the season word and a two-part juxtapositional structure, usually presented using objective and commonplace language. In the West, the Haiku Society of America began in 1968, and there are now thriving haiku organizations in many other countries as well. In the Seattle area, the Haiku Northwest group was founded in 1988 (although greatly predated by the Rainier Haiku Ginsha, for Japanese-language haiku, which began in 1934). The Seattle Japanese Garden often has haiku-related activities, including a haiku contest for its annual moon viewing festival in late summer or early fall each year. Numerous haiku journals, such as *Modern Haiku*, *Frogpond*, and *The Heron's Nest*, are published regularly, and the Haiku North America conference has been held biennially since 1991 in various cities around the continent, including Port Townsend, Washington in 2005, and at Seattle Center in 2011 (with the banquet up the Space Needle). The California State Library in Sacramento also houses the American Haiku Archives, the largest public collection of haiku literature outside Japan, founded in 1996. An online search of these societies, publications, and organizations will help you find more information. Further reading online or in essential books such as Cor van den Heuvel's *The Haiku Anthology* and William J. Higginson's *The Haiku Handbook*, and, more recently, Jim Kacian's *Haiku in English: The First Hundred Years*, will help to inspire you to write some haiku of your own. The word *haiku* is both singular and plural, and haiku poems typically avoid titles, rhyme, and overt metaphors and similes. Haiku also tend to avoid initial capitals and closing punctuation because they are fragmentary and not complete sentences. Haiku may look easy to write, but it's challenging to make them work well, without artifice. As Seattle-born haiku pioneer James

W. Hackett once put it, a haiku is like a finger pointing to the moon, and if the hand is bejeweled, we no longer see the moon.

Here are a five haiku by contemporary poets from Washington State:

snapped line—
the salmon's full length
in the air
—Francine Porad

deeper pink
where cherry petals overlap—
my hand in yours
—Ruth Yarrow

spring memorial
the dampness
in a handful of soil
—Alice Frampton

moonlight billows
through a mosquito net
the sound of the sea
—Christopher Herold

summer garden
the full stretch
of the hose
—Connie Donleycott

To conclude, here's a poem of mine that parodies a Bashō haiku about Kyoto:

misty garden—
even in Seattle
I long for Seattle

An Elegant Utility

Inye Wokoma

I live in the Central District, a neighborhood that for most of the twentieth century was the heart of Seattle's black community. This is no longer so. To say that gentrification pushed black people out of their community grossly oversimplifies a long and complicated history which prevents us from fully understanding where we are today. I live in the first house that my grandfather purchased within a year of migrating to Seattle after World War II. It is a home that resonates with the collective memories from seventy years of family life. Because of this, when I am in my home I feel centered and alive. My home is surrounded by five other houses that used to belong to family members; the people that used to live there have moved away. On the streets outside my home I often feel lost. These houses where family used to live are like shells, echoing with ever fading memories. My home is still here, I keep the energy alive, but the community that made it is largely gone. Every time I leave my house I often feel disoriented as I transition between two lived realities: one familiar and affirming, the other challenging and often alienating. Adjusting between these two energies daily makes life feel thick; every movement is studied and intentional. I have chosen to stay in this community and in this home. This choice forces me to grapple with three defining questions: How did I get here? Why am I still here? Where am I going?

Since taking ownership of this home, I began cleaning and organizing my grandfather's workshop and garage storage. As I sorted through his things, specific objects triggered family stories that captivated me. Fueled by those three defining questions, these stories began to embody something

An Elegant Utility, Paccar Gallery, Northwest African American Museum

much larger. I began to understand them as stories of how a specific place, community, and identity came to be.

An Elegant Utility is a collage of recollections and meditations about life in the Central District. It is about what is beautiful, useful and purposeful. It is about passion and pragmatism, holding in the line and pushing the boundaries. It is about tradition, irreverence and the places where the two are indistinguishable. It is about race and land, economics and self-sufficiency, conflict and love. It is about who we imagine ourselves to be and who we aspire to be. It is about how black family was maintained and black community was built, one choice at a time, one relationship at a time. I am embracing one sliver of my family history as an expression of black people's collective struggle for freedom in Seattle. I am telling one version of this story, the story of black resistance and self-determination in Seattle as expressed through the life of Frank Green.

This presentation is not meant to be reductionist in its treatment of black Seattle's nuanced history, just selective and deeply personal. I need my own answers to those three defining questions in order to face the future. I am hoping, in the same way that our personal and collective stories are intertwined, that my process of exploration will be useful to others.

Note: Mr. Wokoma's exhibition, *An Elegant Utility*, is in the Paccar Gallery, Northwest African American Museum, January 28—July 27, 2017 (2300 S. Massachusetts St., Seattle). From NAAM's catalogue: "*An Elegant Utility* explores the creation of place, identity and the Northwest African American community that has historically characterized Seattle's Central District neighborhood. Featuring a collection of artifacts, including photographs, utilitarian household belongings, and legal ledgers, *An Elegant Utility* examines how the personal history of artist Inye Wokoma's familial lineage, the Green family, serves as an entry point through which the larger story of African-Americans in Seattle, is reflected."

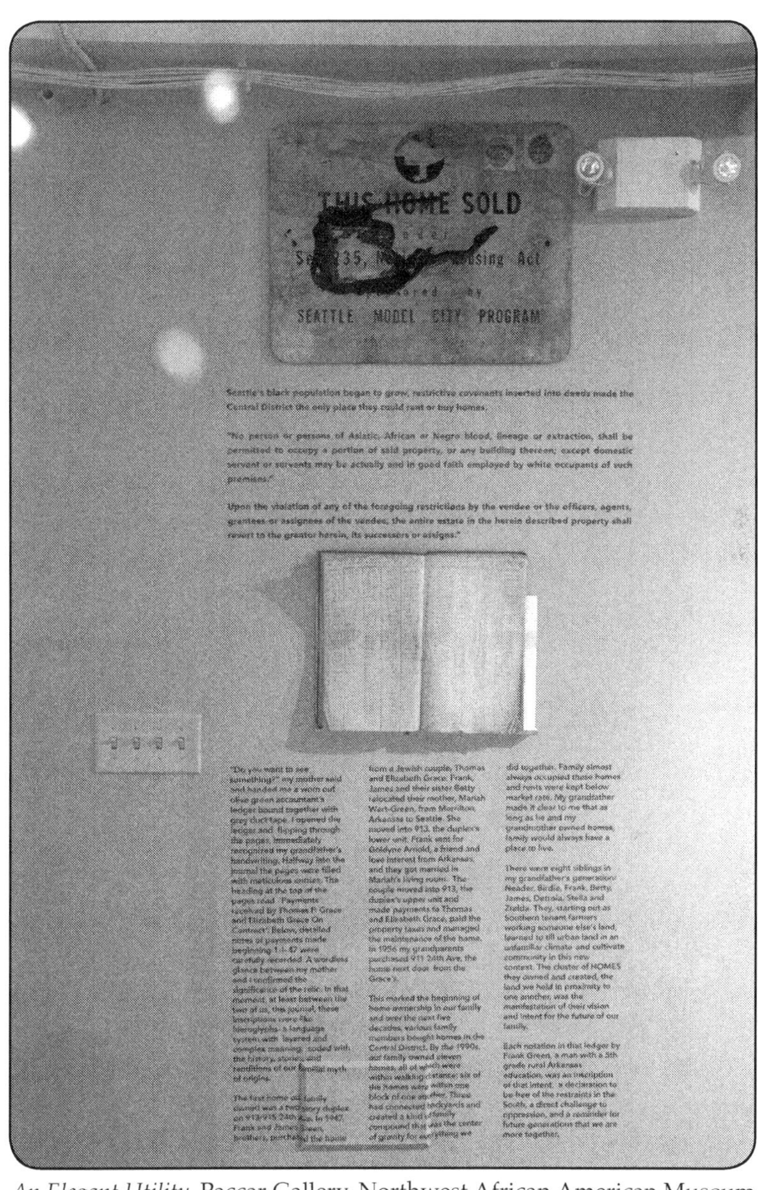

An Elegant Utility, Paccar Gallery, Northwest African American Museum

VII

Spoken Word: Stories We Tell

Women's March #2, photo by Anna Bálint

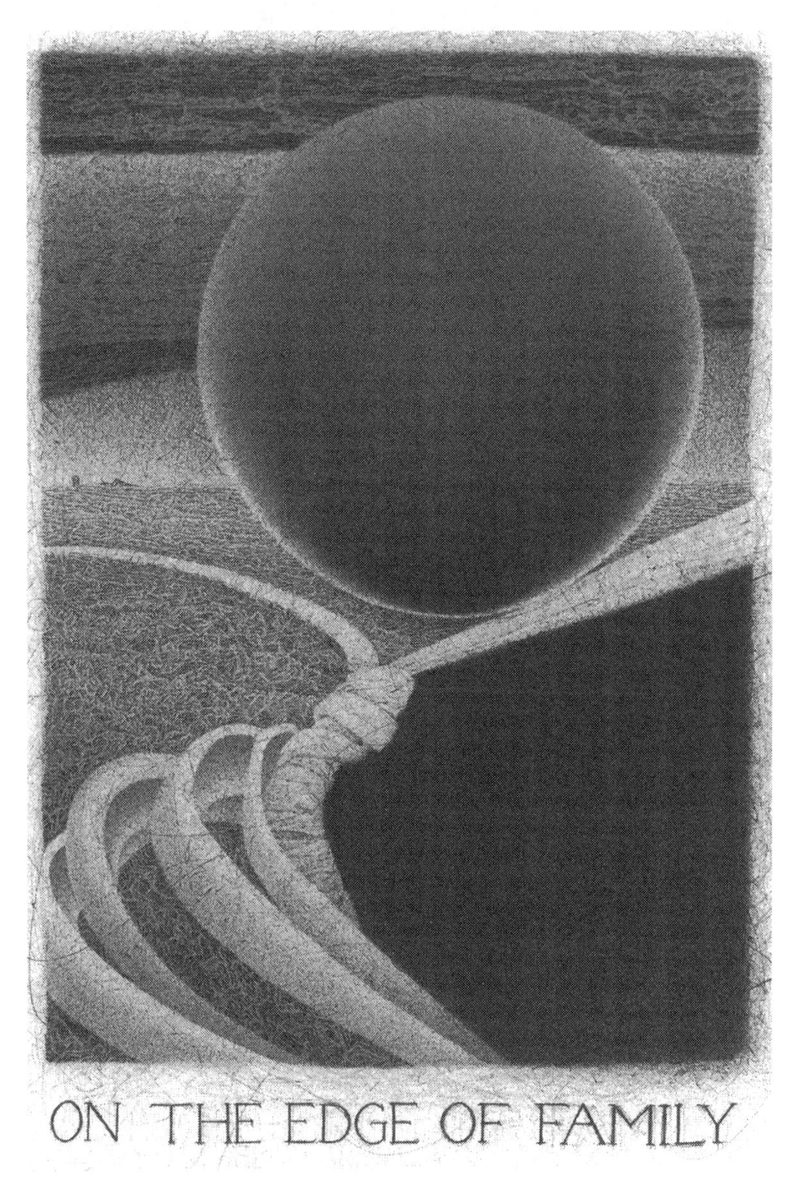

On The Edge of Family, drawing by Robert Ransom

Fetching the rains

Soonest Nathaniel

My father fears to watch his children take to the road,
he fears he might enter a world of metaphors.
He is married to the night,
but I am a bat in love with the dawn.
Father's limbs have grown heavy,
but there is fire in my feet;
I can hear my heart dance to the music of my thuds,
my journey began where his had ended.
Last night I took to the road,
on the path out of the village I met a cat,
but I did not heed its warning;
for life is worth nothing
if not lived in curiosity.

Father says the world is flat,
he warns that I might fall off its tapered edge.
But I say,
"when doves shed feathers off their silver wings,
I will glue the feathers together and take flight."
I tell him I will touch down on the other side,
where seagulls skim over the waves.
Father says sometimes the road turns to water,
And I say
I will grow fins,
I am not afraid to drown;
for this child must learn
to father himself.

I tell father
I know of dead villages,
I know of cremated hopes,
But I do not know of dead roads.
I want to gather new stories,
for a village where peace has died away
like a cigarette in an ashtray;
I go to get new stories,
for a house that lies full,
reeking of tales which lips fear to tell.
I do not long to inherit my father's gods and concubines,
I depart to find a new name.
And when I return, I will come with the rains
to wash off our roofs, the corpses of dead narratives.

It doesn't take a penis

Soonest Nathaniel

I was born by a woman, who sits like a man.
Her legs wide open without fear
for what the prying world would see.
And she will say,
"let them bear witness
that this lady is endowed with an elephant-sized testicle."

My mother wears yucca fibres for sandals
and rabbit furs for clothes.
Her neck is adorned
with shells, stones, bones and dried berries;
and she will say,
"dead memories too are ornaments."

On certain days
she will place my head on her thighs
and with affection in her eyes
she will say,
"big ships drown in pools, ponds and puddles,
it doesn't take a penis to impregnate a woman."

So at the school of her lap,
I learnt to castrate my fears
in faith to fertilize the womb of barren dreams.
Last night I heard her say,
"the open road never dies,
it leads to a lake full of laughter."

Parting ritual

Soonest Nathaniel

When father died,
they shaved my mother's head
to the scalp,
then they forced her to bathe
with the algae-green water
gathered from rinsing father's corpse.
Six yards of white cloth
sewn into a mourning gown,
mother wore a smile,
it was more lethal than a frown.

They forced her to eat,
they said she will need strength,
strength to look the dead in the eyes
and confess to lies,
lies that she ate her husband and his other children.
Hers was a feast of worms,
and though sadness filled her stomach,
she struggled to eat the maggots
wriggling from the ears, eyes, mouth and orifices
of decayed justice.

They let her walk the meadows barefoot,
father's grave had been dug at the end of the grove.
They claim she crossed the thin line
between apples and snakes,
so at the node where two positions meet,
she will light seven candles,
then circle the grave with chalk.

For 90 days,
they confined her to a room,
the "other room,"
where every limp comes to pose as a patriot,
where every screamer thinks himself a prophet,
and every crook claims that he is a statesman.
But after all the lechers and mourners go home,
my mother will rise and make love to silence.

VIII

Featured Theme:

HOME

Home, Hyderabad, India, painting by Srilatha Malladi

Riverside Home, photo by Nyri Bakkalian

unfinished house

Luther Allen

swallows nest in the rafters
of my unfinished house
flit and swerve through future windows
mouths full of insects, chirping, joy.

the flight of humanity
has been much on my mind.
the deadly puerile and penile
wagging of power and territory.
killing from belief, killing from non-belief.
kneeling before the progeny of the hydrogen jukebox*
tossing the nuclear dice.
our lives of pixeled vicariousness
practicing greed as soul work.
our mania for distraction and diversion.
incontinent paranoia and malignant punditry.
the armageddon box-knife of technology.
abandoning the unwashed, the unschooled, the unlucky.

our suffocating fear of the unknown.

where is the phoenix of compassion and love,
the blossoming of enlightened community,
actualized spirit? is the ash of the burned books,
burned villages, burned forests, burned air,
burned bodies, burned minds too deep
too complicated, too hot, too hard?
we seem to be burrowing underneath
in tunnels of clever words, clever things, broken art,
fabricating endlessly fascinating fractals
of the shallow, false and useless.

never really touching, never really knowing . . .

off in the distance i can almost hear the doors
of god's car slam shut, the engine start, then
the tail lights glow dim in the dusk
as it heads down the road to another planet.

* * *

i will somehow finish the house,
the house with such a magnificent and costly foundation.
i will wrap it for winter after the swallows have fledged,
peck away at the siding, run plumbing and wiring,
insulate, sheetrock—crafting the necessary order.
the exterior will be painted a calm and solid color,
the color of wet sand, of listening.
the trim something vibrant and deep, so
passersby will know their knock will be answered.
the interior will be painted the color of infinite sky.

there will be a broad brace under the highest gable
exactly the width of a swallow's nest.

i will somehow make this place complete.
to flit and swerve, mouth agape
to fly up through the ashes.

*From Wikipedia (https://en.wikipedia.org/wiki/Hydrogen_Jukebox): *Hydrogen Jukebox* is a phrase coined by Beat poet Allen Ginsberg, from his poem *Howl*.

"'. . . listening to the crack of doom on the hydrogen jukebox . . .' It signifies a state of hypertrophic high-tech, a psychological state in which people are at the limit of their sensory input with civilization's military jukebox, a loud industrial roar, or a music that begins to shake the bones and penetrate the nervous system as a hydrogen bomb may do someday, reminder of apocalypse."

Some Birds Line Their Nests with Leaves

Dianne Aprile

—For Paul

We took a walk for old times' sake, that long week before I left Kentucky. There, ahead of us on the path, you spotted a perfect bird's nest resting upright in the middle of our route—a tangle of twigs, emptied of contents yet whole and undamaged. Odd ornament flung from a tree. You stooped, swooped it up, held it in the palm of your hand, then turned to me. "This is for you." Reaching for it, I barely gave a thought to how it came to be in this particular place at this moment in time, or to the history of its inhabitants, to the storm or the bandit that dropped it there so blithely. I drove home, talisman swaddled in tissue on my passenger seat. Two houses and thousands of miles later, I keep that nest—small and tight as a fist—in a shallow dish on top of my guest-room dresser. Without any help from me, it's still a tidy house tightly-wound of wiry stem, clots of spit and dust. I study it now and then, recalling that once familiar path, crushed-rock and fossil-strewn. I nod to the memory it revives, and to what is possible and to what's not. I couldn't have imagined the trail I would travel after moving from the only state I'd ever known to this tangled place anchored in promise, lined in layers of leave-taking, my life now. Some days I pretend a songbird sits in it and sings.

Deconstructing a Book

Dianne Aprile

Ravel: unravel, untwist; entangle, complicate; clarify by separating the aspects of.

Books break down over time. They come to life as organic matter, wood pulped to paper, pigment turned to ink, bones of beasts to glue. Over time, they fox. They fade. Sunlight, breath, fingertips nudge pages toward demise. But behind them, in sheaves, they leave traces of their origins, the sweet, the sour, the decaying scent of time.

She smelled of lilac the first time she read to me from the old yellowed book. That's how I recall it. She spent the morning cutting stems, placing them in a porcelain pitcher. When she opened the book and showed me the poem by William Wordsworth, I couldn't have known who he was. What a poem was. What language meant, would come to mean. She read the poem aloud—sunlight searing the room. Breath bathing the book. Thumb touching tongue before turning the page. Each action a step toward extinction.

Over the years, she read the poem often (day, night, spring, fall) until it felt etched to my flesh. Classic Wordsworth. A gentleman on a hike in the countryside encounters a girl, eight years old, and strikes up a conversation. The poem's title, "We Are Seven," refers to the girl's argument that her two dead siblings are still a part of her family, of who she is. The dead don't leave us but persist, no less real for being unseen. The gentleman tries to persuade her that there are only five now, the others buried, gone. No longer countable. She ignores his math, insisting: *we are seven.*

It was an odd poem for a healthy young mother to read to her child of four or five. Years later, when she died, too young—me still in my twenties—it was the Wordsworth poem that called me back to the house with the sofa where we read. I searched until I found the book in the back of a closet. Found her, too; her DNA on the page—knowing it was there though I couldn't see it.

To preserve a dying book, first deconstruct it. Remove its covers. Unlace stitches, loosen leaves. Take note of stains and tears. When your dismantling is done, breathe in the remains. Commit to memory: dust, light, lilac, a girl, what's left of her mother, their raveling bond.

Journeys

Anna Bálint

1)
Pack. No more than you can carry. Hurry.
You have to leave now, tomorrow may be too late.
There is no time to pack!
Run. Run my child, just as you are.

Soldiers appeared in our village.
Shooting began. I lost my brother.
I lost my father and brother. I lost my friend.
We fled into the night, our village in flames.
We spent our time hiding. Our city was falling.
Every day airstrikes and barrel bombs.
A rocket was dropped. My mother was maimed.
The bombs were every day, every day.
We cannot go back. We have nowhere to go back to.
Only the road. Or the trail. Or not even a trail.
Only the hard dry earth. The cruel sun.
Children, barefoot, walking one behind the other.
Mothers carrying babies, walking for days.
Sleeping under a tree. Up at sunrise. Walk,
before it is too hot to walk. Crossing rivers,
fathers holding small children above their heads.
Crossing the White Nile. Continuing to walk.

2)
Look at a map. Find Syria. Find Sudan,
South Sudan. Somalia. See how the Red Sea
separates two continents, Africa on one side,
Asia on the other. Now, trace these journeys:
Syria to Jordan, Sudan to South Sudan,
South Sudan to Uganda, Somalia to Kenya.
See the human rivers crisscrossing the land.

Za'atari, Dadaab, Kakuma, Bidibidi, Nyumanzi
Places of refuge, their names sing of sanctuary.
Za'atari, Dadaab, Kakuma, Bidibidi, Nyumanzi

3)
Do you know of Dadaab?
The world's largest refugee camp and Kenya's
third largest city? A city of tents, population
six hundred thousand. Barrel shaped tents, plastic
sheeting stretched over hoops; makeshift shelters
built from sticks. A city in the sand, sprawling
then disappearing over the edge of the earth.
Inside its gates no warlords, no drought, no famine.
Inside its gates you are safe. Here are your blankets.
Here is your water. Line up over there for food.
Expect to wait. Waiting is an art. You will
practice it everyday and become a master.

In this city of tents you will find hospitals
and schools. Your baby will not die of malaria.
Your children will pursue their education, girls
as well as boys. Here are markets, busy busy
with plenty. Find fresh and canned goods,
soda pop, clothing. Find shops selling cooking
pots and brooms, radios and bicycles.
Here's a kiosk to charge your mobile phone.

And yes, it is true, a fence rings the camp,
with razor wire on top. You ask, why is it there?
Is it to keep you safe from the outside world,
or keep the outside world safe from you?

4)
I am a refugee.
That's my name now. Refugee.

Life is different here.
It's not like being at home.The toilets are dirty
so we don't use them. We go to the bush.
Since we came here, life is not what it used to be.
I want to be in that life before. The good life.
Our house in Juba was air conditioned.
Here there are food shortages. This month
only maize flour. No beans or rice. No firewood
for cooking fires. Last month no cooking oil.

Sugar, morning tea, milk,
these are the things I miss the most.
I miss the breeze and smell of the air in my country.
I miss the flowers on my balcony.
I miss Friday afternoons in my neighborhood.
I miss the olive trees and fields of wheat.
I miss the birds and the harvest season.
Can anyone miss anything more than their own home
and the tree they sit under?

Last night I had a dream.
I dreamed I was back in my village.
But when I woke up I found myself here.
Here there is gravel, there is grey, but nothing
green. No plants, no trees, no grass. Only
the white of the tents, the grey of the gravel,
and the wind. Do you hear how the wind
tugs at the tents? The flap and the snap?

When the war ends we will return
to our country and rebuild our city.
When fear is gone, then we can go home.

5)
Do you see those young boys playing kickball?
Do you hear how they laugh as they play?

They are children born here, boys already home,
three generations of refugees under one ragged roof.
Their mothers and fathers ache from waiting
for a country to grant them asylum. Better to wait
for a boat to a new life. Wait for two days, three,
maybe a week. No longer than that. While you wait,
look across the water and dream. While you wait
for a boat your brother in Berlin waits for you.

The boat when it comes is an old fishing boat,
its motor is not good. The boat when it comes is
an inflatable vessel too flimsy to cross the sea.
The boat when it comes has a rusted hull and
sits low in the water. Too low. So many boats.
So many people. So many children. The weather
worsens, waves toss, and blue water turns black
under stars. Morning when it comes is a mist,
the only color the orange of life vests, the only
sounds the chug chug chug of the motor,
the slop of waves, and a baby crying.

6)
Dreams:
A new country. A house. An apartment. A room.
Someplace to come home to. A place with walls,
windows and a door. A stove. A table. Some chairs.
A bed. Two beds. A TV for the children. Maybe a balcony,
a place to step outside and take some air. Who will be
your neighbor? Will they welcome you?

Dreams:
The place you left behind. The place no longer there.
The place that in your memory still exists and will exist
forever, untouched by bombs, unchanged. The courtyard
still there, waiting for you. The smells of the kitchen,
warm bread, onions and meat frying. Outside, a tree

heavy with lemons. The lemons will always be there
in your memory.

7)
You have waited. Today your turn has come.
Today someone in uniform calls your name.

Forms, photographs, fingerprints, interviews. Documents scrutinized, backgrounds checked. Where were you born? Where did you live? What city? Why did you leave? What is your education? What is your occupation? What is your religion? Do you have any diseases? Open your mouth. Say *aah*. Step on the scale. Take a deep breath. Where is your wife? Where is your husband? Why isn't he with you? How old are your children? Where are their birth certificates? Do you speak English? Look at the camera. Look to the side. Turn around. Take a seat. Wait. Come back tomorrow. Come back next week. Expect to wait at least six months, a year, two years. Longer.

8)
You have waited. Today your turn has come.
Say goodbye to the elderly mother you must leave behind.
Kiss her, wipe her tears and promise you will send for her.
Then journey once more, this time by bus or by train.
Beyond the window, unfamiliar landscapes flash past.
Maybe you will board a plane. Your child sits on your
knee. Buckle up. Is it really safe to fly so high?

9)
A new life is hard to start, but this is where we live now.
Come inside. Look around. Rugs with bright designs cover
the floor; there are many cushions to sit on. Make yourself
comfortable. I'll pour you some coffee. It's strong
and very good, the way we make coffee in my country.

Outside is a satellite dish and family laundry hung out to dry, pants next to skirts, next to shirts big and small; purple next to pink, a sudden splash of red. Two little girls wearing headscarfs zoom past on bicycles. Where are we? Are we in Frankfurt, London, Seattle, or Rome? Are we in Jordan? Is this the Za'atari camp? Could this be Beirut? We are somewhere now. Newly started somewhere. Have we arrived? Are we home?

Western Red Cedar

Michele Bombardier

The dark-eyed juncos wait in the cedar boughs,
patient for the chickadees to finish at the feeder
near the dining room window which I open to fill

and they pause, green-grey heads tilt,
eyes straight into mine, we are eight inches apart,
only glass between us. *They know you*

says my teenage son, watching, the one with the life list,
who asked for *The Sibley Guide* for his thirteenth birthday,
read it under his covers by flashlight.

We built this house three decades ago,
under the boughs of an old-growth cedar,
Giant Arborvitae, Tree of Life, old survivor;

and me, a new mother from a home that crackled
with violence, learning to nest, to brood
over her young, to change flight.

I go outside, pull the deck chair to the sill and wait.
Sure enough, soon sunflower shells spill into my hair.
I bow my head, grateful, and receive them.

The Visitor

J. R. Robinson

Good night! Good night! As we so oft have said,
Beneath this roof at midnight in the days,
Thou hast but taken thy lamp and gone to bed,
I stay a little longer, as one stays,
To cover up the embers that still burn.
—Henry Wadsworth Longfellow

Grayson visited William once a year. He didn't come to haunt him. He didn't try to frighten him. Nor was he interested in revenge. He owed no debts and held no grievous sins that forced him to walk among the world of the living. He came, entirely of his own free will, to pay the man a visit. No one ever noticed that he was there, and when he departed each year, he left no trace of himself behind.

On the anniversary of his death, his ghost materialized inside the walls of the familiar home. Darkness lay over the house like a heavy blanket; to Grayson it felt the same as daylight. He walked through the house, just like he had when he was alive, gliding silently through the halls as he peered at the hundreds of photos hanging on the walls. He always felt silly when he was floating in unfamiliar territory, scenes of Casper the Friendly Ghost flitting through his mind. Here, however, where his memories beckoned to him like an old friend, he felt comfortable enough to let his feet touch the earth.

A loud whimper as he walked past the nursery provoked only a grunt of dismissal. Grayson wasn't obligated to care about children that weren't his own. The bright sunny dreams flowing out of the room didn't appeal to him in the slightest, so he simply ignored their existence. Children were nasty little things, after all. Grayson walked proudly, as if he were still alive, though with more freedom of movement compared to his previous flesh and blood body. When confronted with a closed bedroom door, instead of hesitating, he smirked triumphantly, then melted through the wooden portal.

His intense yearning to descend upon William faded once he entered the room, as usual, and Grayson stopped in his tracks. He was here. He never gave a second thought to the compulsion that dragged him from one side of the universe to the other, following him through layers of sorrow, anger, and regret. Every year, he rushed through the walls of this house, into this room, and stared at the lumps lying side by side, unrecognizable under their thick blankets.

This man. William. And his *wife.*

William. The name reverberated through him as if he still had a physical body, as if his bones were still hollow, as if the name were a gasp of oxygen coursing through his blood, through every step that had led Grayson to him. The dark shadow that represented his soul rippled due to their proximity to each other, as if someone had skipped a pebble across his shimmery surface. The emotional discord made him feel . . . *alive.*

He was familiar with which side of the bed William always slept on. He let one knee dip into the soft mattress, and as usual, he hesitated to continue. His past had ceased to haunt him ages ago, but he still felt a twinge of pain in his heart every time he came near this man. But why else would he be here, if not to prove to himself, year after year, that William was alive and well? He had always felt responsible for this one, from the moment they met as children to the moment they became comrades in the midst of war.

He had saved William. No. Actually, William had saved *him*—The ratty, ugly, unfortunate orphan with no family or friends. A boy with a loathsome personality that rivaled the nastiest of men. The boy who proudly wore his failings as a thorny shield against the world. William was the only one who had tried to reach out to him, stubbornly suffering under the pain of his thorny barbs, unafraid, always a bright and forgiving smile on his lips. William had been his best friend. His *only* friend. The last thing he'd seen before he died had been *William*. No wonder he kept coming back here.

His obsessive thoughts about the wretched man had brought him back to his bedside, every year. Sometimes he watched from the corner of the room; other times, he sat at the edge of the mattress while his fingers ghosted along the sheets. Grayson scowled as he watched the bodies shift. To his eyes they emitted joyful radiance, brightest wherever they happened to be touching. He barely glanced at William's wife, a glimpse of her long blonde hair prompted fickle memories of jealousy and dislike. It didn't escape his notice that there were actually three heartbeats under the warm scrunched-up blanket, although he could hardly qualify one of them as a person. Yet.

Hard at work, are we? Spawning more little brats.

The thought burned in his mind, the flames coursing through him and coiling upwards in the pit of his belly, like a serpent ready to strike. He wanted to shake the man, violently. Every new life created with this woman carried William further and further away. From their past. From him. Each new child changed the man, made him happier, and each year that passed made him less the man that Grayson had once—

What? *Loved*? No. Protected? Yes, that was an acceptable word. Protected would do.

Eventually, the day would come when it wouldn't be worth crossing over to mingle with the living. On that day, Grayson might finally forget that he was dead.

He stood there, suffering under the heavy weight of William's presence—every minute spent near the man brought back another long-forgotten memory. Grayson stared at him for so long he noticed he'd started to breathe. That irritated him. His incorporeal body was trying to copy the hypnotic rise and fall of William's chest. The man was irresistible, but then, so much about the perfect bastard tended to be.

The man lay exposed under Grayson's intense scrutiny, face relaxed, a bit stubbly around the chin, his shaggy brown hair curled and twisted upon the pillows. Without his thick glasses, he looked almost—Grayson racked his brain for a word that wouldn't embarrass him or give himself away. "Innocent?" No, not exactly. Not "beautiful," either. Hah. William, beautiful? What a laugh. William spent too little time on his appearance to be considered that. Alas, Grayson was too distracted to come up with a more convincing description.

Struck by a sudden sense of greed, he ran his smoky fingers through William's hair. Grayson wished he could feel the soft strands against his skin. He lowered his face until his nose was inches away from the unruly mop—did he still use that lemon-scented shampoo? When he was still living, Grayson would often tease him about smelling like cleaning supplies. If only he could smell him now, just to check if there were at least *some* things that didn't change.

"Ah," he shook his head as if to reprimand himself. Hopeless hope, this wanting business. A sign that he still couldn't let go.

Fuck it. His fingers slipped down the side of the man's face. It was stupid to stroke him like this—he wasn't a fucking *dog*—but he did it anyway, solaced by the fact that none of it really mattered. He could no more feel the silkiness of his skin than he could enjoy that crazy nest of thick hair. William's eyelids twitched. Grayson froze like a thief caught in the act, convinced his uninvited trespassing had disturbed the man's peace.

Surprisingly, the soft glow surrounding the bed brightened, and for just a second his whole arm was bathed in it, revealed visible, his hand delicate upon William's brow. Warmed by the sight, Grayson leaned in even further to kiss the spot where his fingers rested.

Wait.

Had he gone *mad*? Had he lost all good *sense*? He stayed frozen in the position. Beneath him William shifted, and under the glow of the light, he saw the man smile. *Oh.* He kissed his slightly-parted lips instead.

Terrified, he bolted upwards. William had felt it. Hadn't he? Grayson was almost certain the man had. Dear Lord, what was he doing? He was *dead.* The afterlife represented acceptance and the release from worldly pains and desires. Did he really prefer an eternity of despair for what could have been? Regret in reliving lost chances? To hell with that.

"Hmm," William murmured, twisting his body over and thrusting his backside toward the edge of the bed. Grayson stood up, trembling, feeling his spirt, his soul, shaken once more with this terrible craving. He wished he couldn't *see.* Couldn't *think.* Couldn't *feel.* Anna Sunley—oh yes, he knew *exactly* who lay wrapped in William Moore's arms—rolled onto her back with a sigh, and after a brief struggle William's right arm untangled itself from the blanket and wrapped itself around her bulging stomach.

"Shhhh," William whispered, fingers gently splayed across her belly. "It's alright, little one. Go back to sleep. Daddy's here."

Out of nowhere an icy blast of air rushed at Grayson like a frenzied blizzard. His already wavering grip on reality flapped around him like dead leaves, his mind scattering in a thousand different directions, but he refused to be shoved out and discarded like yesterday's newspaper. Fuck that. He'd find himself back on the other side if he gave up now. Tumultuous in the night, his hair and clothes billowed violently, soundlessly. He could feel the wind dragging across his body, clinging to his molecules and sucking him backwards. *No,* he didn't want to go back.

As he struggled to maintain his grip on the world around him, all he could focus on was: he's *awake.* William's awake.

He had never woken during one of Grayson's midnight callings. Clinging to this reality with all his might, he bent down. The light dazzled and warmed him as he submerged his face into it.

William's hand moved slowly, a steady, loving caress. Hovering over him like a spider ready to drop from the ceiling, Grayson watched as William pet his wife's pregnant belly. William wanted this child. Truly *wanted*. That was clearly obvious. Obvious, and yet that was something that never occurred to Grayson in the past: some parents loved their children with an unconditional strength. Some parents cared for their offspring even before they're born, before knowing anything about them. His stare was intensely focused, unblinkingly so, on William's movements as he traced the swell of his wife's body.

Grayson's eyes blurred, forcing him to blink and break the spell of the moment. When he cracked his eyelids open once again, he found himself staring at William's mouth. "Hush, hush," William whispered, his voice warm and comforting. "Be a good little boy, Grayson. Let your mother get some sleep, she's had a long day."

Grayson?

There are thoughts that can take you from one place to another. But there are certain words, spoken out loud, that can call to you as if you've been waiting to hear them your entire life.

Grayson would never allow himself the comfort of lying down on the bed. Good Heavens, no. He wasn't here to dream, to fantasize about what might have been. He didn't crawl over the covers, didn't clutch at the blankets with all his strength, and didn't settle into a sleeping position. As far as he was concerned, he hadn't moved an inch from his spot beside the bed.

Yet, there he was, lying right next to William. The mattress underneath him. He on top of it. Somehow, he had ended up stretched alongside his body, shielding William's back from the cold night air, his head resting carefully on the pillow. Utterly astonished, he pulled his face from the tousled hair at the nape of William's neck, and wondered what the hell just happened and what the fuck was he supposed to do now. The vortex of wind that had tried to drive him away from the bedroom had died out, leaving him calm and relaxed. Unlike his mind, his body knew exactly what it wanted, curling around the man like a touch-starved cat.

As William inhaled, so did Grayson. He felt no desire to force himself off the bed. Its occupants had no clue he was there, dark and dead, full of yearning and bitter, fierce longing. Something inside his chest shivered, but he remained still, like bark on a log, determined not to disturb the man's peace. Anna coughed and moved about restlessly, and William said, "Shhh," his fingers stroking gently. "Quiet, Grayson, you'll wake your mom. I can't wait to see you either, but it's not time for that yet, okay? Quiet, little one. Be good and let her sleep."

Grayson's nonexistent throat muscles clenched together tightly, nearly choking him. He wanted desperately to chuckle. Even more so, he desperately wanted to press his lips against the crook of William's neck.

"Listen, my son," William whispered, "I just wanted you to know . . ." and his voice vibrated through Grayson as if someone had pressed their mouth against his ear and hummed deeply, a static strangeness that blocked out all other feeling. "We will always love you. We'll never make you feel as if you're unwanted. We'll never make fun of you. Or call you names. Or make you cry. We won't dress you in hand-me-down clothes or keep you from making friends. You'll always have enough food to eat. You'll have—"

William's voice snagged, and without a second thought, Grayson wrapped his entire body around William like a warm coat. William swallowed thickly, and Grayson felt the movement from the top of his spine all the way down to the edge of his toes. "You'll have the childhood he never—a lot of us—never had."

Grayson rested his face against William's head, inching himself closer and reaching out to rest his hand on top of William's. He wished with every inch of his soul that he could feel *something*. That he could comfort, and be comforted, with the brush of his thumb against William's knuckles.

Never in his wildest dreams did he think that someone would—*wanted to*—name a child after him. That was an honor far beyond anything anyone could ever bestow upon him. The act was so unexpected, so beyond his belief, beyond anything he'd ever experienced, that he couldn't bear the thought of having to let this man go. Not again.

He could feel something. Startled, Grayson raised his head and listened. He heard it. Dear God. He could feel the heartbeat of the little boy who would one day replace him. The child who had yet to enter this world.

He and William lay that way for a long time, hands joined together, Grayson's darkness disseminated by the light around the bed, all four of them quiet and peaceful together.

If only he could stay like this forever.

But . . .

He didn't belong here. Not just in this family bed, but in this room, in this house, here in this world. He had to leave.

To his surprise, when he tried to disentangle himself William instantly scooted backwards, pressing up against him, following after the memory of being held in his arms. Confused, Grayson caught him around the waist, and William shook his shoulders free of the heavy blankets as if to allow himself more physical contact with his ghost. Grayson held on tighter, wishing he could offer him more.

Beside them Anna stretched her arms and let out a contented sigh, and William's hand rushed through his own, reaching out to make sure she was all right. After a certain amount of groping and shifting about, Grayson was amazed to see that William's hand traveled back upwards and found his again. William's fingers curled around his own, sliding in-between with confident certainty, as if Grayson's hand was real and solid flesh.

Grayson remained where he was for the rest of the night, unmoving, just holding William Moore, his hand quivering with the steady beat of the baby's tiny heart. Once dawn neared, Grayson finally breathed out a sigh of relief and let his body relax. Tucking his face into William's messy hair, he closed his eyes and smiled for the first time in many, many years.

In the early morning, when the bright beams of sunlight washed over the bed in brilliant flames, the baby kicked and his parents marveled once more at their son's impatience to be born. It was a wonderful morning. A normal morning with just the three of them. As if no one else had ever been there at all.

Back Again

Elizabeth Burnam

I remember the rope that cradled me.
I remember the itchy arms, rashes
dug into my wrists, and yet it held me.

I remember the bruise that remained, cool
like a lover at my bedside, sorely
caressing me awake from a sweet dream.

I remember the cage, tall as heaven,
wide as the burning train, lurching toward
an uncertain horizon, panting smog.

I remember the violence and the pain,
only the pain, unperturbed by prayers
softly spoken into my own cupped palms.

I remember gasping in the moonless
night more acutely than I remember
squinting my eyes at the rising sun, but

I remember that the sun did soon rise.
I remember the train station, crowded
with proud-shouldered passengers who came

from foreign lands with all their foreign pain.
I remember the end of suffering,
stretching, jetlagged, glad to be back again.

seriously, dip pen & India ink on paper, by Clare Johnson

Time Traveling on Creston Street

Jennifer Clark

When a smaller box s *is situated, relativity at rest, inside the hollow space of a larger box* S*, then the hollow space of* s *is a part of the hollow space of* S*, and the same "space," which contains both of them, belongs to each of the boxes. When* s *is in motion with respect to* S*, however, the concept is less simple . . . .*

—Albert Einstein, *Relativity and the Problem of Space*

Honest-to-God tiny tumbleweeds of dust, cat, and dog hair roll across our feet. The realtor's mouth is moving, his words garbled in the musty air. My sister and I travel room to room, where unfinished or poorly executed projects loom. Here and there, walls slashed opened, we avert our eyes, try not to notice exposed insulation, fuzzy pink tongues hanging out in surprise.

Stepping onto the sunporch that melts into a screened porch that hardens into a walled-patio where, in the middle of this open house, I stagger over myself sunbathing with the neighborhood cat, Clarence, dozing on my back. My sister disappears but not before handing me a sledgehammer. My father arrives and side-by-side we rage against the concrete walls. My father, in his white t-shirt, translucent from sweat, causes the house to tremble. Tomorrow and three houses later, he'll stumble playing golf, fall at the ninth hole and hurt his knee. He'll refuse ice.

Oh, here's my sister, curled on the couch sleeping, nestled next to our grandpa who's smoking a pipe and watching the Detroit Tigers. Our brother has just flown in from Spain and is playing with blocks. We're all falling asleep. The risk of falling into melancholy mounts until my mother, wearing a fashionable wig and looking like Mary Tyler Moore, runs down the stairs. Instead of singing, *Love is all around, no need to waste it . . .* she's screaming lyrics not quite so catchy, something like *damn it, I'm nobody's maid. I wish I had become a nun and never given birth to you.* For the chorus, she throws clothes, shoes, a hairbrush, books, a box of Girl Scout cookies—Thin Mints—out the front door. All this damn stuff doesn't stop people from piling in, these people that can't see we are always dusting here on Creston Street.

Our dead Chihuahua dashes across the room, my brother not far behind. *This house is one hot mess* a woman says, eyeing me as she heads downstairs where period underpants soak in a bloody pail. Somewhere, a floorboard moans.

Now we're emptying plaid beanbag ashtrays that float away to eBay. Bathroom mirrors we clean each week until they squeak while some other ghost of a family flecks the mirrors with dried spit and toothpaste.

Open the linen closet and they're all there, the same endless exchanges wafting through the house. The sweet, syrupy voice of Jean Nate whispers into Dorothy Hamill's Short & Sassy Shampoo. The green, no-nonsense bottle of pHisoderm off by himself while the too-piney Clairol Herbal Essence claws at the Tussy deodorant.

Folding in and out of itself like a bellowing accordion, the fabric of time is pleated. I'm ten years older than my mother who is shaving her legs in the bathtub. I open the Emeraude, the cheap little bottle that dared live on after my grandmother's heart stopped beating. My grandmother rushes from her grave. Flush with death, she puts on a Tom Jones record. *My my my Delilah . . .* We dance past my mother who never became a nun and always bore us. She's wearing an apron now, Bermuda shorts, and no wig because she's tossed the wig along with her walker into the air. She's stirring Hamburger Helper on the stove, my sister at her side. We are all so happy, my mother without her walker, her undead mother, my sister, and me. We could all be friends.

Renaissance House, illustration by Michael C. Paul

Blue Christmas

Cheryce Clayton

"Jeffy, put that down!" Momma shouted again. It was blue. Christmas wasn't supposed to be blue. Jeffy remembered Christmas, it was red and green and happy with candy and food and presents. Everybody laughing. Singing songs. Watching TV.

"I said put it down!" echoed through the trailer and Jeffy glanced at Momma to make sure he had two more warnings. Sometimes she lost count and punished him on three.

Momma was sitting with Gramma at the little table, smoking and talking, mostly smoking while Gramma talked, and tearing apart toilet paper balls to destroy the makeup smears. There was a pile of shredded paper in front of her and almost no makeup left on her face.

The shiny balls on the tree were blue. Frosted in places and hung with little metal hooks. The tree was solid white and made out of plastic snow stuff that felt itchy when Jeffy ran his good hand along a branch. The blue ball he had taken off the tree was the same glass metal everyone else's Christmas balls were, only blue. A faded winter sky blue with lopsided snowflakes painted on.

Dad liked real trees, big trees, trees that they went in the snow to hunt and bring home. Covered in dark red ribbons and deep green balls that picked up the lights and big red and white candy canes for the sneaking.

Jeffy scraped his thumbnail against the frosted snowflake and watched it crumble off to reveal a brighter shade of blue.

"Put it down, damn it," Momma said behind him and Jeffy moved around the tree a bit, so he could watch her and Gramma at the table and still explore. That was four and sometimes she moved really fast at five.

Jeffy was five. That's why she gave five warnings. She used to give three, he didn't remember her giving four warning, but he didn't remember being four. Only three and then the hospital.

He remembered Christmas before the hospital, Dad took them to the swimming pool hotel. They went to a party with Santa, and all his presents were wrapped in Rudolph paper.

Jeffy cupped the blue ball with his dead hand and reached out to pull a metal thing off of the tree. It was old, rusty and pitted in places, but still mirror shiny down its length. It was twisted, and Jeffy thought about putting the ball down to try to untwist it, but a glance to the table got him a frown from Momma. He put the metal thing back into the tree. It fell when he let go of it, sounded like a wind chime, and he reached out to take a second one and study it more.

The Christmas tree at the hospital was green plastic and didn't looked real. He wondered what it felt like, but he never got to touch it. It had red glass metal balls and little plastic Rudolphs like his wrapping paper, and hanging plastic glass icicles. Gramma told him they were icicles. Told him she had icicles on her tree. Never told him her tree was white or her Christmas balls were blue.

The old icicle was just metal like a pop can torn up. Jeffy tapped it against the blue ball. He tried to be quiet so Momma wouldn't decide it was five times. The metal made a light tink and the ball broke, pieces falling onto the single present beneath the tree.

Jeffy watched as tiny red spots appeared on his hand, cuts. He wanted them to hurt. Like things did before the hospital. So he could cry and Momma would come and hug him and give him a sucker.

But the cuts just bled. Large red drops falling onto the box he had helped Momma wrap for Gramma. It was a toaster. Jeffy loved toast and he wanted Gramma to have toast so she could be happy for a little while every morning like him.

Dad used to tease him about toast. Say the toaster was

broken, claim he had to eat cold milky cereal, or eggs.

Toast was perfect. Crunchy, almost burnt, with just a bit of butter. Even the hospital let him have toast. And Jeffy ate it every morning, even when they burned it. Like Dad.

The broken blue metal glass ball looked green from the inside, and Jeffy dropped the pieces onto the present. The Rudolph wrapping paper caught his blood drops and Jeffy set the second metal icicle next to the first, before carefully reaching into his pocket and getting a tissue to press against the cuts. The way Momma would have, before the hospital. Before the fire. When Dad was still there.

"Here, honey, let me," Gramma said.

Jeffy flinched, expecting five. Only Momma was gone. The trailer was quiet. Gramma knelt beside the white Christmas tree with the blue balls, and Jeffy didn't see any tears or hate in her eyes as she helped him press the tissue against the scars and stop the bleeding.

"Let's go find you a lollipop," Gramma said in a whisper.

"I'm going to be six," Jeffy answered.

still February, dip pen & India ink on paper, by Clare Johnson

Living Alone

Mary Eliza Crane

I become quickly accustomed to living alone
small simple meals
hummus and figs
spinach and eggs
rice, a few slices of cheese.
I no longer track the comings and goings
of not yet adults
piles of shoes
plates on the counter
sudden changes of mood.
There is never a full load of laundry.
The well does not run dry.
Baths are long and luxurious
hot and scented
patchouli or cedar in salt.

I lock the door at night now
like a woman who lives alone in the woods
at peace with the wolves
but not so sure of the hunters.
I slip into cool sheets
and drift into twilight sleep.
My lovers are old men
face cradled in soft chests
of gray bristling hair,
a mirror of uncluttered want
communion of pure need.

Cool House

Minnie Collins

I am on the rim, near the edge
Zigzagging most harried days
Trekking daily back to my hope place
My shelter, a relief from storms, rain, snow, and wind

Welcome to my living room
Here in this space are heroes, myths, blues, and ragtime
  that speak for me
Coffee, tea, Coke or day-old treats for the asking
Even much needed naps after miserable nights out
Of course, you have to smoke outside.
Freshen up in my bathroom: face wash, underwear change,
  tissue rolls free

Yet here in this place, restless, unnerving, trouble maker
  sometimes am I
Shaking conventional guests
Who decry me as lazy, restless, not good enough,
  dangerous
My haven is hope for the misplaced, lost, overdue,
  spine broken, or brand new
My hope haven has no hierarchy, no privilege,
  no discrimination
My haven accepts me just as I am
My haven welcomes all
I persevere; survive in a really cool house:
  the Rem Koolhaas Seattle Public library

Dining with Mexican Jesus

Larry Crist

Back when we were still a family, dining
out meant this one Mexican restaurant
with a moat of chickens round the door,
small children playing quiet in the corner,
family run, waiting on us, working the kitchen

I'd order a hamburger that came in a red plastic basket,
potato-chips, a pickle, a thin red onion wedge,
lettuce, tomato, sweet as any we grew
My father would order a saucy mound of goo
called the special
and my mother, something small and slight
like her, a la carte

I didn't know anything about Mexican food
and little about Mexicans themselves

I'd see them in the fields on the way to school, ask
my father why these people came to do our work?

They used to own this state, he'd answer, *before it was a state*
before we took it away.
Why'd we do that? I'd ask.
Same reason we took it from the Indian, he'd say, *because of gold*
and because we could.

Kids littler than me played naked in open yards
beside old trucks with dropped engines, cars on blocks
Laundry connected one kennel-sized shack to the next

In school they were polite, spoke English, dressed nicely,
neat in any case. The girls wore tiny crucifixes
and pierced ear posts

With harvest complete our class size would swell
then with spring closing in it emptied out again

They were hard to make friends with
A single family might have a kid in every class
They'd gather on the playground, the older ones
scolding their siblings if they had gotten dirty
or played with gringos. I tried to make friends
as long as winter lasted

My father would order a second beer, mop his plate
with a tortilla while my mother made conversation
She was a bad cook but could always stir up conversation

A bright narrow poster of a matador was framed
beside the door, plunging his swords into a bull
A colorful illustrated map of Mexico and its flag
alongside a bleeding tortured Christ bound by cross,
a crown of thorns on his head. My parents explained
this was the Mexican-style Jesus, as opposed
to the kind I was used to seeing

It was special eating something not your own
My chin to the red-white-checkered tablecloth
Mother and father seated at the table unlike home
where I ate alone in front of the tv

Music wailing, a somber accordion, a bright mournful
tuba, torch-singed phrasing, sad without knowing why
or what was being said, only that it was very very sad

Here in the California wine country
up from where we lived
this foreign place
that smelled like home

Ceremony of Rending

Jenny Davis

The most beautiful place in the world
is a grove of trees in the hills
of NE Oklahoma
between a waterfall
and 2-acre-sized ponds.
It was not easy to leave
those woods. 12 years ago
I performed a ceremony of rending
the swaying of my boughs
shifting ever stronger against the soil around my toes
but the red clay gripped firm and
no amount of twisting could loose it.
I threw my weight east and west, then north and south
until the howl of ripping trunk from roots
tore through the night.
There was nothing left to do but
cut off my branches
to move quicker across land and water
peel off my bark to write letters
for people who will never even see my grove
burn my leaves to keep warm in far-off winters
carve myself into a pole that would separate twins.
Stand me in the ground and
I will point your way
I am always leaning home

In Search of Home

Risa Denenberg

From Rittenhouse to Juliette, Marietta to Sequim,
I've grown tomatoes on fire escapes, sketched
maps on kitchen cabinets, pinned post cards on walls,
only to leave hundreds of tiny holes when I depart.

I always depart. Things don't work out as planned.
I clash with the boss and get fired. My lover
takes a lover. I feel hemmed in and need to escape
the hundreds of tiny holes in my heart.

The hole in my heart makes its absence known.
The doctors are not hopeful. I refuse to cry, as long
as I still have time to sing sad ballads, to mourn
lost mornings and my hundreds of tiny blunders.

The huge and tiny blunders, kitchen to kitchen,
bedroom to couch. If I don't pine away right now,
I'll join the old folks who sit at card tables holding
paper cups, swallowing hundreds of tiny sips.

Life is a bowl of tiny sips from which I have glugged
my share. What seems to loom large is, after all,
only one short life, this teeny-tiny stint of time
to partake, to embrace, and then, to depart.

History Lesson

Patrick Dixon

When you sort it out alone
you become weightless,
at the mercy of whatever mean wind
rustles the corn.

You spend the time
holding your breath.

I drag out
brittle photos,
beaten journals,
bad poetry,

words frown
from decades past,
surge at me out of a dark
I turned a long shoulder to,
so I thought.

I fill with water
that rises
to a boil.

Remember?

Of course.
Long nights
under the bed
with dust-ball spiders;
behind a locked door—

flies buzzing the window;
scramble to a basement corner—
dirt floors and crumbled masonry,
where a shadow walks past the crack
at the top of the stairs.

It Is Over There by That Place

A Remix of English Influenced by the Loss of the Native Language

Diane Glancy

What can I say? I am assimilated. I don't have native language. I am reclusive. I don't have documentation. My great-grandfather missed the Dawes Rolls. He fled Indian Territory because he was in trouble. He spent his life hiding in northern Arkansas. My great-grandfather was full-blood Cherokee. My grandmother, half. My father, fourth. Myself, eighth.

What I have left is a visage. A printer's drawer without the letters of the syllabary in the sections of the drawer—as if in the Old Territory where the Cherokee newspaper, *The Phoenix*, was printed. I use splayed sentence structure and layers of meaning outside of English composition taught in school.

What is there in history but a shape of being? A language structure that is *place* with its multiple meanings of places within place.

***

I translate without original language. I translate the traces of the process of original thought. Something of what says other things—

My first memory I remember was the sun through the curtains in a moving breeze moving the sun. I was in the crib. I am when no one else, it said. The curtains my mother bought. Not made. There were all these words in the word for the place on which the house sat in which my room was in the house. Next to neighbors. Not open land, but housed in neighborhoods. The city where I lived.

A distinction of what I was in the relationship to parents. To them there belonged no one similar. They were the ones who were parents. I knew they came into the room. I liked father. The mother was disconnected from the room. I was in the crib they bought. She had nowhere to go on her own. But her with him went those places to buy.

The sun kept coming through the curtains. Connected to where I was placed. There were shadows moving light from one to another light. The light where shadows not covering it. But moving. Light one place. Shadow another. Was where the fingers went. The shadows of the places that moved in the light. Migrated across.

I would be hurt. That was known. It was in the words the place carried. It was in the description of what it would be. It was part of the word that meant place where lived. They had been hurt where they came from. He from a longer journey. She from a shorter one, but which she took longer.

I was in a crib. The sun came through the curtains at the window. The sun was outside the window. The light was sheer. The curtains as if gauze. There was breeze that made the curtains move with shadows in the light. They were disrupted. Moved by breeze. Was I cold? Was it a summer day? Where was my mother? Not wanting to come into the room. She does not want to come. I am not liked by her. It was part of the conjunction of the places on which our house sat.

They were away from their place of belonging. They were trying to make a new belonging where they were. It was not working. He was something of which she was not. There was restlessness sometimes in the shadows. They were ungrounded. These words for them was not known. Being. Meaning. Knowing. There were places in the land that carried words.

The fingers on the hand followed the shadows that were there. They remained in that place though moving. The shadows hid the sun. Then the shadows let the sun. It was there and it was not there.

The language his family had known was gone. They were called evangelized. They went to church. I was taken with them. There were straps and sinews in every word. Sometimes it boiled up in loud words.

It is over there where it happened. The land calling from where it said. From what it breathed. From where it walked. Where it happened was known by the intrusions there. The old window shade rolled up with a cord and ring-pull round as the sun.

My memory of the sun through curtains moving in the breeze from the window came into the room—crying before maybe of starkness. Shadows from the slats of the crib a forest of trees in straight lines. Woodland was the street where the house was.

Where it happened they were walking. They spoke of knowing. Over there by that place. They spoke of being. It belonged as similar. No matter where. It would be land that stayed land. What of necessity—of it saying what was. The minute it came was long ago. It was unfixed. With someplace other than its place to hold.

Later large clouds rolling over the land flat as the crib with trees in the distance was the land there. More to there than what was there. Otherwise the bleakness of one part spoke. It was shadows moving the light to another light where shadows not covering.

In grade school English composition interfered. To empty pockets of other thought from it. To somewhat it did. But they remained—if they stayed flat. Otherwise I was in trouble as he was in trouble. The city where I lived—Kansas City, Missouri—with the name of another place of which it was not but bordered on part of it was.

The Last Ferry

A rengay by

Penny Harter, Tanya McDonald,
and Michael Dylan Welch

that distant island
there, not there
morning mist *Penny*

the loon disappears
mist on her glasses *Tanya*

mist obscures
a black dorsal fin
winter rains *Michael*

threading shore pines
a valley of mist *Penny*

heavy mist
a seagull feather
rides the current *Tanya*

the last ferry home
missed *Michael*

Midtown, photo by David Anderson

The *Next* Place is Home

Thomas Hubbard

Kids in my neighborhood played touch football in the street, filling the afternoon with arguments as they learned valuable negotiation skills. Summer evenings resounded with shouts and noise of more than a dozen of us playing "slips," a rambling team tag game we played on our bikes. We'd choose up sides and one side would chase the other until they were all tagged, ranging through driveways and backyards, onto the next street over.

Sunny summer days, the girls sipped sodas and pretended to read novels around the huge municipal swimming pool, the bold ones sporting bikinis as they gossiped and watched the boys jump or dive from the "high dive." On rainy days we played board games on somebody's front porch, or hung out at the YMCA. A few times we got into making model airplanes, the ones made of balsa sticks and covered with super-thin paper. Lynn, who lived a few houses down the street, always set his afire and sailed them from an upstairs window.

At an intersection about a mile from my neighborhood, five streets came together. The area immediately surrounding was called Five Points. I attended junior high school with kids who lived around Five Points, and we often hung out at a little restaurant nearby. We would sip Cokes and play the jukebox and cheat the pinball machines. On warm evenings we sat on a stone wall at the five-way intersection, playing "dozens." This was a rhyming game, making fun of one another's families. It required a certain skill to "score" without getting into a scuffle.

Some of us found part-time jobs as we entered adolescence. I worked evenings as a pinsetter in a bowling alley.

That was hard, dirty, sweaty work. Leagues of men or women had five-person teams. They rolled three games, one team to each lane. A pinsetter would set two lanes, meaning thirty games each league. At eight cents a game that made $2.40 in an hour or so. The factories paid only about $2. I sat two leagues a few times a week.

Downtown boasted department stores, movie theaters, pool halls, and a Carnegie library. I read hundreds of stories in that grand old cut-stone building under the watchful eyes of librarians who tried their best to be forbidding. Anytime I asked for help they would turn into sweet old aunties.

At the edge of town, a gigantic factory made automatic transmissions for Fords. My older cousin lost the middle finger on his left hand working there. Another factory built Chevy transmissions. Across the street from my junior high school, a huge foundry produced cast iron transmission cases for cars and trucks. Three blocks away the world's largest glass container factory made bottles and jars, and the boxes for shipping them. My dad worked there, and helped me get on when I turned eighteen.

After a couple years doing labor I began my apprenticeship in the family trade, making glass bottles and jars. It was magic, if you could stand the heat and noise. I'll never forget the older guys, like old Bill Stringer and Dago Favors, who so patiently taught me to operate a machine the size of an average living room.

The machine was made up of five identical sections, in line, each one doing all the operations necessary to change a gob of molten glass into a pickle jar or a whiskey bottle. The machine sat under a fire-brick trough running molten glass (above 2000°) to a "feeder" that streamed the glass out through a ceramic disk with a precise round hole, to be cut into drops by carefully timed steel shears, synchronized with the machine. Each section had a scoop that reached out at exactly the right instant to catch one drop of glass and send it down a chute into the mold.

The iron molds had to be swabbed every ten minutes or so with a mix of graphite and oil to keep the white-hot glass from sticking. Bill Stringer taught me how it had to be done on the fly, in perfect synchronization with the whole machine. Each time the swab touched a moving mold it would puff fire and smoke. Swabbing was like a dance. All the constant adjustments of cooling and timing of the machine had to be done without shutting it down. Another dance.

But the main part of the job, as a beginner, was watching the bottles pass on the conveyor belt, and spotting even the most minute flaws. And then adjusting to correct them. It seemed, at first, as though I had to be working on the machine in the back and front, and watching every bottle, all simultaneously.

After about a year I had the job down enough to get by. Then Dago Favors, the "feeder man," taught me how to crouch in the tight little space above a machine and reach around the stream of glass running free into the basement through a hole in the floor, to change the shears and ceramic orifice on a feeder. Dago could look up at drops of glass flowing out of the feeder and tell the temperature of the glass. He was a round old genius with greasy spectacles and an engineer's hat, who talked funny.

But things were changing. The bottle factory closed down and I moved to Los Angeles to finish earning my journeyman card. As a member of the international union, I moved from city to city, soon becoming a troubleshooter and setting up new jobs. The money was good, and almost every city had a glass factory. For seven years I didn't think about home very much. And then, due to my "bad habit" of reading fine literature, I decided to quit the glass trade and go to college. Thanks, Mr. Carnegie.

Back in my home town I earned a degree, tending bar at night. I'm pretty sure it was an "outfit" place. A lot of secret, after-hour dealing went on, and occasional poker games with pistols laid out on the table. They let me lay off when

I needed to study, and welcomed me back because I was fast, the register was right, I didn't drink, and I "didn't see nothin.'" The owner, Bucky Huff, may have been shady, but he sure helped me through college.

Bartending showed me the depths of ignorance but education introduced me to the sixties' alternative realities. My cousins, uncles, aunties, and grandparents came to view me differently. Whenever I spent time with family, I felt like a visitor. I had to watch what I said. It hurt them to see me going beyond their world . . . to "lose" me, as Mom said years later. It was as though I'd betrayed my roots. In some ways, I had.

School was fun and bartending paid well. Then it was over, and I was the first college graduate on either side of my family. My home town was dying but I didn't notice. I was teaching writing and literature—I had made it.

Being a teacher and a coach took every waking moment. Meanwhile life went on. As the shine wore off my teaching career, I moved into writing magazine articles for a living (and sometimes working construction), then migrated to the Pacific Northwest where I taught again, using my working-class background to gain cooperation from troubled kids . . . until retirement.

Retirement made me want to own a home, so I bought a cabin in the Ozark hills, in the middle of the country. Almost everyone there plays guitar, and they're *good*! And Ozark friends don't fade.

After significant time in a place, working and making friends, leaving may *seem* easy because the next place beckons. In truth, we leave a part of ourselves in each place. These parts of myself that I've scattered about haven't let go of me. They call me back again and again.

So now I travel to Seattle and down the coast to Los Angeles and across the mountains and desert, sometimes to Chicago, and all in between, driving straight through and sleeping on couches or in the car, visiting everywhere. At least once a year I visit my Midwest home town. But it's not my home.

All the factories disappeared. Downtown died. Raw, weathered plywood covers the windows of many businesses and houses. Neighborhoods on "my" old side of town are run down, with trash in the yards, junk cars in the driveways. Where factories used to run day and night, weedy vacant lots remember better times. The schools I attended are gone, replaced by housing developments already seedy and declining. Here and there, amateurish repairs and gaudy paint. I cruise the town, a tourist. Always, the *next* place is home.

Tom Tripped On A Loose Stair And An Angelic Choir Sounded Like Falling Rain

Tom Hunley

Days after he wrote
the biggest check of his life
(a down payment on a stone house
with four bedrooms, a great unfinished basement,
and a porch covered with snow
with no shoeprints but his own)
Tom tripped on a loose stair
fumbled a box of books
hit his head on the cold concrete floor

He loved the way sunlight glinted
off the window
—his sunlight, his window—
loved all the empty rooms
like books he hadn't yet written
loved the silence and the darkness
which arrived and brought the moon
loved the little beer fridge
the basement's only furnishing
loved the ice cold Old Chubs Scotch Ale
that he rescued with outstretched fingers
loved the warmth of blood clumped in his hair
and the otherworldly light
that formed a staircase with no loose stairs
and the voices of angels that sounded like falling rain
arranged into the song he'd been seeking everywhere
the song that finally made sense of everything

Death Means Going Home

Tom Hunley

"Going home without my burdens / going home behind the curtain / going home without the costume that I wore"
—Leonard Cohen, "Going Home"

Tom died far from where he
expected to die
thousands of miles from where
he was born
unlike the salmon
who return to spawn and die

All of his weary travels
tore this life from him
peel from an orange

He died in the dark, his hands
not recognizing the hands
that held them

He died with red marks on his wrists
where handcuffs had chafed them
though he couldn't remember his crimes

Do you remember hearing
your favorite song for the first time
or living, for the first time,
in the pages of your favorite book

Dying, Tom C. Hunley had this smile
on his face, adopted orphan
seeing home for the first time

and bicycles, dip pen & India ink on paper, by Clare Johnson

The Valley

Clare Johnson

The barn looks like it is about to fall over. It has fallen over already. It is at the bottom of the lake, it has been splintered by the river, we have no memory of its owner, its owner has probably drowned or left town. We are very few. We all have barns like that. We all used to have them. The school teachers and ranch hands pass through with no possessions, they must be related to someone who changes with the seasons. My best friend took a picture now but said it looked different through the lens. I was expecting it.

It is a valley and I think of it as flat but it's not really flat. There are little crests and hills with new houses on top and no yard. Even the main highway has ups and downs. It would be hard to jog all the way to town. I don't think of myself as an athlete. In truth, I've given up trying to make you understand. The houses are falling down the hills, maybe like a joke from a book you buy at the supermarket. Who made them. Why do they stay white while the barns are sinking to the bottom and grey.

There are towns now, and a summer crowd and skiers. We can feel them somewhere, maybe behind our backs or clustered in the trees, up the mountains in expensive jackets. They take pictures that won't turn out. They are here somewhere. I gather up my coat and feel invisible and wintered. I will get mixed up in all the seasons, I have seen it. I know there are people here. I have been told it and seen that I have relatives somewhere. These are my mother's old sewing projects.

It is a valley and it took a long time, I am starting over. It took forever, everyone was hidden or late. The last place.

Telephones came before electricity. There was one at the hotel. That's not even a town anymore, who remembers those names, there was a hotel there though I swear it, with grand porches and a telephone, no yard only dust or grass or someone's grey suit on Sunday cutting into the yellow. There is a street because the houses are in a line, this is how it looked when I read stories as a child, I imagined covered wagons, those buildings out of nowhere. There is nothing but the porches. There must have been people somewhere, but I don't see them in the photograph. I was expecting you forever. Were you planning on staying?

On the far end there is the mystery of hills to someone who is only visiting, the trees still, the deeper lake, the remnants of the glacier, the real lake, much colder. The other end is river and leaving, as if you could really leave quickly, it travels down and there is a road now so you don't have to worry, don't cling to him like that anymore. It trips down regardless of the weather, I am freezing or sweating, don't do that, LET GO OF HIM, you can see the old road cut into the hill, the wagons and the rocks below. Like something urgent or your summer vacation. That man you knew in St. Louis who left and never wrote. Maybe you found a letter the other day, maybe you only imagined it.

Take my hands and stop looking over your shoulder, follow the river up farther and follow its current with your eyes, clasp that bag close to you but for God's sake let go of your sister, walk behind me, walk behind me, I am leading you through the dirt and dust, I am leading you next to the water and you must never go in, I am telling you to take my hands and keep them with you close, I know we are from the same place despite the worry where your eyes should be, we are from the place where my hands and face and feet are going to be like dirt or just red and bloodied, I believe you are going to come with me and get thinner lips each year, each year my hands will be what you recognize and followed behind me like a dog, a bolt of fabric into dresses for this time, we are traveling with the river and losing our hearts to it, I don't need longer words for you or the blisters on my heels, just stop looking that way and you look so mournful, let go, we are almost there, the rocks in your shoes scattering and WE ARE ALMOST THERE the river climbing and disappearing into a valley, the yellow grasses now, the first barn I ever knew sliding into oblivion.

Beginner's Guide to Failing

Sarah Jones

Be born into a family of drug users.
Watch your dad roll joints, drink beer,
welt your mom's cheekbone.
Find white powder, glass, and razor blades
in your mom's purse.

*

Eat cold cereal alone some nights for dinner.
Tell your mom to get out of the bathroom
with that gun—tell her not to kill herself.
When she accuses you of sleeping
with your stepfather, run from the house.
Take shots of tequila with LeAnna
until you pass out. Start keeping
a bottle of Jack behind your headboard.

*

Let LeAnna's older brother who's home
on leave take your virginity
on the floor in front of a glowing
space heater.
When he asks you to stop crying,
try to be quiet.
Believe God will forgive you.

*

Let the nine guys after him
have you however they want.
Ask yourself if they could give you
love, if they will adore you.

*

Listen to your stepfather say
how much you look like your mother.
Look into a mirror and see
a white face too old to be yours.

And one day, my shadow will walk away

J.I. Kleinberg

Show me the place that is safe enough for silence,
the furnace that burned the memory from stone,
the shell that listens to my ear for the echo of truth.
Fingerprint on the mirror, my reflection smeared,
a threaded road inscribes my face, my palm.
With ruined broom, I sweep scrabbled shards,

confirm my incomplete metamorphosis,
this slow grooming of death I do each day.
Every word is hidden within the same curdled letters.
Every moment turns to look back over its own shoulder.
What have I gleaned from the raucous warnings of crows?
Where shall I place the tokens of this languid forgetting?

The afternoon moon peers through the open door.
My throat aches where the song left it.
There is no pill for this wound.
Even the stones weigh nothing.

Apartment

J.I. Kleinberg

A humble place, my apartment
is appended to a squat stucco house
where my noisy neighbors slam and yell.
Past black calla lilies through the gate
follow the broken concrete walkway
to my little yard hemmed by cinder blocks,
soil turned and bare but for a row
of tiny green marijuana sprouts
planted by Raymond, who lives next door,
as if I might not notice,

and a tree—a can-can dancer,
leg kicked high to show pink petticoats
layer on frothy layer.
If you're quiet and no one's throwing
plates against the wall that afternoon
you will hear the low buzz of bees and
smell the flowers.
I like to stand right next to the trunk,
head in the blossoms in the day's heat
just breathing the noisy sweetened air.

I don't know it yet but Raymond's friend
will slide two louvers from the window,
then slip through that skinny opening
above the kitchen sink to steal
my camera and my favorite red Reeboks.
The police will dust the window sill
and sink and doorknobs with black powder

and when they catch him I will appear
in court, my hands held apart to show
the judge how narrow that window was,

and he'll say *please describe it in words.*
But the camera and shoes are gone.
I don't know it yet but that summer
the pink flowers will become hundreds
of nectarines, a fruit I've disdained
for not being a peach, and which I,
intoxicated, enamored, will consume
still tree-warm, glossy ripe red,
the juice running down my chin into
the recently trespassed kitchen sink.

The Gates of Vietnam

Gina B. LaLonde

It's Friday night and Jorgian Spitt is inside the Gates of Vietnam. Building 108, Boylston Avenue, Seattle, Washington, United States, of America, yes. But her courtyard, the deciduous swampland it's become, is a land of snakes and razors, of lush and bile: Vietnam is what Jorgian will know this courtyard as, even twenty-three more years from her twenty-third birthday—which the clock is just wrapping up—as will her neighbors; her neighbors that lie tightly tucked, enveloped within the Gates of Vietnam.

From a monk's crouch on her mildew-infected floor tile, Jorgian watches the courtyard through her window. It's been a dull evening, the kind Jorgian has taken a liking to in recent weeks. A silent birthday this time around would be perfect. But she knows this is too much to ask. From her perch, she watches Vietnam with a hunter's eye. She can feel herself hovering over the gates where mud mixes with more musky mud as the April 18th rains swell the veins and innards of Vietnam. Not even a firework bloated in gas could ignite in such downpour. This thick mud is Vietnam's blood, the rain an omnipotent force that pumps the heart and keeps Vietnam breathing; the spirit, or God in a way.

Jorgian then turns her attention to Vietnam's skeletal system, Building 108: the edifice glows with jaundice lights peeking from worn velvet window curtains. Gray soviet bloc façade, the apartments spread in a confined kidney formation, guarding the sweetbread organs of the garden. Jorgian listens. A shattered-glass elevator creaks floor to floor, dinging in exclamation and yet traced by irregular bouts of stringent laryngitis. Jorgian avoids riding it at any cost, knowing that it could be this capsule's final rise or fall, either leaving her trapped in the bubble or plunging deathward-bound into the deep cement cavernous girth of Vietnam's underground parking lot.

With the building still standing, Jorgian springs to her feet and quickly moves to her bed, knowing that this quiet will part like the velvet curtains on the windows of Building 108. She has a strange feeling. The complex will be a jungle tonight, as figures hover above and figures hover below. Deep night takes hold, and from her bed, she peers out her window and—smells the demon that the trespassers should beware of.

She inhales, taking in the rains. Leaves sag like aged breasts. An onion, discarded from someone's putrid Quality Food Center bag just blocks away on Pine Street, grows its own family of others just like it; a reincarnation of opal and pungent proportions. Jorgian knows it's vital that this onion succeed in its rebirthing life-cycle; if this decrepit organism can make its way in the field of Vietnam, then so can she.

"So can we all," she whispers, lazily soaking in the foreboding surroundings of the complex from her glutinous second floor window.

And in this overrun moss, palm, and fern-filled courtyard, voices begin to stir—to bounce through the rain, off a puff of smoke, off an angry thump, off a deep moan, off a shrill laugh. She hears it all; the neighbors fucking to the beat of a song above her—

She turns and says are you alright?
I said I must be fine 'cause my heart's still beating
come and kiss me by the riverside,
bobby says it's fine he don't consider it cheating

These cries lull Jorgian to the breaking point of slumber, but not yet. Maurice screams from down the hall at Luie-Skunk outside the gates of 'Nam.

"Use it next time fucker!"

To which Skunk shouts at 'em, "I bent my key or else I coulda' got in myself."

Jorgian lays flat on her bed now.

Will I be okay? Will I wake up? Jorgian needs to know. Then Vietnam ignites. Things begin to happen.

A group of boys, on the hormonal-brink of teen, play men on the iron gate locking in the swamp-like tomb of rot; white slick sneakers sliding, bending at will. Who will be the first to fall as they scale the gates of Vietnam? Jorgian springs up in bed, watches and hears them skip and slip, bend and pour their tiny skater brains out. Then metal pops in the night air. SLAP as blood tears through the skull of the last tightrope walker to fall. Through the dark and thicket, Jorgian sees him, the kid's acne pocks mark him as thirteen at most. Jorgian knows this is what it means to have a shaved head, to eat shit like you for breakfast, to die hard, to remember nothing, and always be walking along that iron-bottomed and chain-link-topped fence outside Vietnam.

Jorgian hears sirens as they stop a skateboarder's rumble. The man in the halfway house across the way claps over and over. Relentless techno crashes through another screen door, and a government paycheck blows through the wind and smudges itself as an inky blot against Jorgian's window. She laughs at the burst of humanity.

Then more claps from the halfway house. Another tight-rope walker tumbles. The other felons from the halfway house burst into a responding laughter. Jorgian synchronizes her laughter in her bed, sitting in a stiff ninety-degree position. Over the mountain pass it would be crickets Jorgian will hear while drifting into slumber. But for now it's the sounds of the city that will have to lull her. TV's, intercoms, buzz-ers, frowns, all things dismal, these are my things divine, she rationalizes to herself as the neighbors moan in ecstasy above and below. There will be a day when things change, a promise to herself, alone.

* * *

Jorgian has fallen asleep, allowing the railing where the boys fell to whisper to her in dreams and prayers. No telling how much time has passed. And then a scathing MEOW resounds that shakes both the building's and Jorgian's bones. She wakes, unable to determine the source of such an atrocious sound. There are small cats that permeate the floors below Jorgian. Not kittens, but little tiny cats. During the summer they urinate on her neighbor's shredding carpet, foul beads sweating in sun-faded, mutant orange.

She's called the cops twice that year just because of the cats. Last June Jorgian had seen Mr. Flank skipping along the cracked asphalt towards Vietnam, his left foot delightfully spry, his right foot tainted with malevolence. Mr. Flank was a buoyant and proud halfway house man all the neighbors were used to because of his ruddy skin and distaste for "gutuppies—gutter trash yuppies." He was all toothless smile.

"You're happy," Jorgian had exclaimed, a little of his lightness rubbing off.

"The cat's gone," he said with joy and the finality of an eternal soul at peace. Back during that night when Jorgian's shivering neighbor Estie came over for Tupperware in the rain, she told her what Mr. Flank had done with the neighborhood stray. Into the dryer, alone, tumbling around until the heat cooked the cat alive.

"Her fur musta' smelled like melting litter," Estie cackled.

Jorgian felt a sad desire to have been there, a part of such a cleansing.

And now, the cats that were spared are getting louder and Jorgian sits up, propped on her back elbows, still in the dark. It seems the cats have picked this night to avenge the stray's death, all having smoked their catnip rocks at one time; the sound of them screeching ominous, haunting, and painful. The MEOWS penetrate Jorgian's eardrums. Their frequency, their chosen decibel so sickly in nature, an attempt to kill all living things that it may reach. Jorgian holds her hands over her ears but is unable to keep her ear canals free of the feline sirens. Then she recalls what she learned at the Indian rehab program at Thunder House, that when cockroaches die, they put out a pheromone attracting all the other roaches to come eat its remains, down to the micro-skeleton. Like cockroaches—if you kill one, a thousand more come to its funeral—couldn't cats be the same way?

That's it. We'll attract every tiny cat in the area, wrangle them in and then . . . Her goal will be to catch them, box them, and send them away to a final resting place of ashes and dust, fur and bones melted down: every last tiny cat. Instead, Jorgian finds herself drawn towards the light switch, but then reconsiders and walks back to bed, leaving the room pitch black. Maybe I can get a few hours of shuteye first. Then. Then take on the tiny cats.

She recalls with a rather half-hearted yawn, I asked a cop to taze the cats once. She wondered if that made her a sick person, like Mr. Flank. The officer only said in return, "You shoot a person, you're in trouble. You shoot a kitten, you're fucked."

"But these aren't kittens!" I protested. "They're tiny cats!"

* * *

In the morning when Jorgian wakes, she dresses and ventures outside with a Saturday haze that has seeped into her muscles. She glances across the street, into the sunlight; rains ceased. None of the halfway house men stand outside smoking and staring. No Mr. Flank. No cats roam. No skateboarders grinding sandpaper boards along the rails of Vietnam. She walks into the street, looks carefully from left to right. Jorgian moves back through the gateway of Vietnam. The swamp has risen in tide from the night's previous downpour.

She wades through Vietnam to get to the dilapidated elevator, which she takes back to the second floor, breaking her ban on the mechanism. Nothing seems sacred or halcyon. For Jorgian, only silence rings loud and clear. She knows all she can do for the time being is wait for what plague Vietnam might bring her next.

Checklist

Charles Leggett

Storage rented; condo emptied, scoured;
carpets and the dishwasher replaced;
washer / dryer serviced and repaired;
oven cleaned; the toilet fixed; new shower
door; listed, primped and prettified, then sold.
The proceeds, given that the dissolution
remains as peaceable, will see division
in equitable terms—for that we hold
out hope. Hope stands aloof but ready, bridesmaid
waiting for the tight bouquet to fly;
stands furthermore perhaps for this blank latter
third of a life beneath the serenade
of a belatedly expiring sky
in what blue modes may make it seem to matter.

Night Train

Joan McBride

This is the long pull
through Montana
as night settles over the Great Plains.
The train fans endless
fields of wheat and barley
and causes jack rabbits
to hurdle away. We pass
a pile of rusted and twisted cars
like an untended war memorial
on a forgotten field.
I haven't seen a house for miles,
or a truck on the road.
This is a stark landscape and
the train speeds up past
this vacant twilight place.

But now the darkening softens
the endless rows of crops
planted as straight and defined
as highway lanes.
In the moonshod landscape
they are dark ribbons
extending to the curve of the earth—
to the border—where the stars begin.
And the occasional farmhouse
with the back-porch light on
is just an isolated galaxy
caught briefly out the window.

Homecoming

Marjorie Maddox

And maybe when you arrive—
stumbling up the cracked path
thick with hopscotch chalk and weeds—
a stranger will answer the door,
insist you're no longer on Elm,
that this is not your home.

Autumn will well up, swell in the gutters
you cleaned every year since twelve,
spill into the color of a landscape
you can't see but feel,
bricks untwining, ivy crumbling,
smoke unbraiding from clouds.

Maybe then you will turn
away from the echo of a knock
back into your own life,
away from my picket-fence memory,
framed still in this dilapidated doorway,
wondering who you are.

Photographic Memory

Kate Miller

Finally home, she sits in the dark car, listening
to the ping of the engine cooling, rain hammering
on the roof. Rolling down the window, she smells
cedar, wood-smoke, wet earth. Leaning her head
back, closing her eyes, she sees the six-point buck
by the side of the road, his eyes just beginning to
film over; the possum dragging its crushed back
legs into the bushes, baring needle-sharp teeth in
a grimace, the dead garter snake slowly turning
itself inside out, the ladder of spine laid bare.

She wasn't there when they took her father off life
support, didn't see him blackened, bloated, lungs
breathing, heart beating, no longer there. She wasn't
present when they turned off the machines, stood
round his bed in the silence, released. She doesn't
have that image the rest of her family carries, staining
their memories. She can see him now, on the deck of
the Alaskan ferry, eyes squinting into the sun, binoculars
slung around his neck, hat brim turned up, laughing.

What We Miss

Kevin Miller

Hatred consumes the news,
what we pass off as hope
appears to be whiskey
in the baby's bottle.
I return to 1990, Grenå's
cobbled walking streets
on a shopping Saturday.
Lines at the Post Office
buzz with people waiting
to pay for phone and power.
frimærke, frimærke, frimærke
I practice the word for stamp
with *til USA* to follow,
the part I have down.

In town, the rush of fresh-
ground coffee greets me
before the cheese wagon,
each works the offshore breeze.
Our kids are kids missing all day.
We have a list, backpacks, and hours
to listen to locals in the midst
of their lives, to love our place
away, to find joy in the simple
wedge of Klemensker, a cheap
red or white we will carry home
for our one obligation to sit
on the banks of the *å* to play
What do you miss?

Immigrant Life in Bohemia

Shankar Narayan

Each day I rend the bones
of birds that never flew.

I cannot touch another body
because of how currents
frighten me.

I do not think what my skin might become
when I twist the throttle.

When I see airplanes or Kalashnikovs outlined
against outlines of towers on sky I
do not think of my death.

It took me a long time to love this starvation
body, these unending arms
without flesh.

Some things I can bear
separation from. My stranger says

I am bones, sees
my boxers hang without touching
my limbs. She means

I am too thin
but when she willfully and with abandonment
swallows my black shivalingam

as holocausts of dismembered beasts retreat through me
she carries me to almost uncontrollable
tears. She finds the chakra

I'd tried to hide. There she is

in fleets of swifts
in my flayed skin
in the free sun.

I cannot touch her verses
for fear nothing beautiful
will ever happen again.

The Promise Broken, drawing by Robert Ransom

The Trombone

Don Noel

"Ole Buttermilk Sky." He didn't need the music; it had been Marv's Scarves' trademark song. Not written for the trombone, but a great tune. He closed his eyes, tried the first few bars. Amazing. Sitting on a park bench, the morning sun rejuvenating his withered face, eyes closed, a tune he hadn't played for what, fifty years? "Ole buttermilk sky, I'm a-keepin' my eye peeled on you." Halfway through, he peeled an eye to the April sky.

A kid was watching him.

A *schwartze*, maybe only fifteen, but strapping, as tall as Marvin and twenty pounds heavier. Standing a few yards away. Contemplating his next move, probably. Just as Marvin had tried to tell Dora might happen.

Dora and Max came to live with him when Rachel died, and a lot of his belongings went to the attic to make room for a new young family, adding to two generations' clutter already up there. The young couple's joining him, just as he and Rachel had moved in with his widowed Mama, carried on a tradition.

If he'd known the neighborhood was going to change so much in ten years, he would have sold the house and helped them buy something in the suburbs with a space for him. Who has a crystal ball?

He found the trombone this morning. His attic trip was occasioned by the arrival of a second child, reducing his private space to what Grandpa had built as a guest room. It had a bath, and was big enough for his furniture, but lacked a floor lamp for his La-Z-Boy. There had to be lamps up there, relics of redecorations.

That simple errand turned into a nostalgic hour rummaging and reminiscing among the detritus of his childhood and marriage in a space redolent of ancient leather, paper, and dust. And there was the trombone, in a dented case, folding music stand tied to it with rotting string. A few sheets of music were inside.

Swing music was still popular when he was in high school after the war. With the longest arms in his class, he was recruited to learn trombone for the orchestra. By senior year he had his own pickup band, Marv's Scarves because they wore red bandanas, playing at *bar mitzvahs* and even grownups' parties. He developed a style emulating a left-handed Negro star named Slide Hampton.

Which showed that he had nothing against African-Americans, as they liked to be called now. He had Negro combat buddies in Korea, and plenty were customers of his hardware store over the years, although none happened to become personal friends. Nice people, if you got to know them—and picked the ones you got to know. Like anybody else.

The neighborhood had by now been abandoned by the Jews and Catholics who coexisted here comfortably for decades. The newcomers seemed good people who got up and went to work every morning and were pleasant when he met them on his walks; Dora and Max knew some of them. The other side of the park, though, was taken over by people who'd been cocooned in housing projects and emerged without having learned to be good neighbors. Half doing drugs. Well, not half, and not all from projects, but enough that you couldn't be sure who was who.

He brought a lamp down to his room and took the trombone to the kitchen. It was tarnished, but a few minutes with the cleaner Dora used for copper pots made it glow. Back then everyone lubricated with Pond's cold cream spritzed with water; the slide was sticky with gunk. He took it apart and washed it as best he could without a flannel snake. He didn't have to ask Dora for cold cream—if women even used that any more—because there was a dropper bottle in the case. *Superslick,* the faded label said. It came on the market about when he gave up the trombone and went to college. It still worked fine.

He took the trombone to his room and tried a scale. Immediately Dora was at his door. "Papa!" she hissed. "The baby's asleep!"

He sometimes found it hard to believe this handsome blonde woman was his daughter, except that she looked so much like Rachel, especially at angry moments when a scowl puckered her eyebrows and her eyes blazed. "It's my old trombone. I played it in high school."

"Fine, just not in the house. Why don't you go across to the park?"

"The park? I can't play my trombone there!"

"Why not? It's nice weather."

"What are you, *meshugenah*? It's an antique. Some *narkotnik'er* could grab it."

She eyed the trombone. "It may be old, Papa, but that doesn't make it valuable."

"It's brass. Even the metal is worth something. They steal metal these days."

"Papa, it's nine a.m. No one's there. Only mamas with babies."

When he reluctantly came across the street, he had to admit Dora was right. Not a *yungerman* in sight.

For a neighborhood park, it was big, three blocks long and two wide. He chose a bench facing the grassy expanse where he'd played baseball, growing up. Nowadays straight ahead was a cricket pitch for the West Indians. Soccer nets up to his left. To his right, a basketball court where kids in baggy shorts and designer sneakers played rough, after-school sport. His only company now, though, were two preschool *kinder* playing on a slide and swings fifty yards away while their mamas chatted and rocked baby carriages. They looked up when he played the first notes, then went back to gossiping.

He looked over his shoulder. The park trees just planted when Grandpa built the house had grown into a wide forest margin, oaks and maples budding out, white birches incandescent against a punctuation of dark green pines. He could make out the house, but Dora wouldn't see him even if she were trying.

The kid, unsmiling, had a round dark-chocolate face and close-cropped hair with a part shaved into it. Marvin's white hair was long, so thin that parting it would be pointless, and it would offer no buffer against a crack on the noggin. The kid wore glasses. Not sunglasses, not designer-chic, just ordinary horn-rims. Maybe thought that made him look studious. Marvin weighed whether grabbing the glasses in a struggle would help. He abandoned the thought. If this kid was a *ganif*, let him just snatch the trombone and run. Make it easy for him, not get hurt.

Giving a noncommittal nod, he made himself close his eyes and play "Ole Buttermilk Sky" all the way through, finishing with a little slide tremolo. He looked up again. Still there.

"Hey, mister. Can I try blowing your horn?"

Sure. Hand over the instrument he'd just rediscovered, maybe a collector's piece for all he knew, and find himself chasing a *tsenerling*, a teenager who wanted to sell it for a fix or whatever? Hollering "Stop, thief!" to an empty park? He'd said "mister" politely, looked innocent enough, and hadn't snatched the trombone when Marvin played with his eyes closed. Still, you never knew these days.

"It's a trombone, young feller," he said. "One of the rules is you never play on someone else's mouthpiece." That was true. In high school, they'd used their own mouthpieces when trading instruments. Avoiding each other's colds, but making adolescent jokes about clap. And that was before AIDS. Can you catch AIDS from spit? He couldn't remember.

He took the funnel-shaped mouthpiece from the top of the slide and held it up for emphasis, "Sorry, I don't have a spare." He put it back in, heavy white metal against the thin brass of the instrument, put his lips to it, and forced himself to get into the music again. He cast his mind back, reaching for a Tommy Dorsey tune: "Sentimental Journey."

He dared to close his eyes again to make the notes come, trying to hold the trombone loosely enough that he wouldn't suffer a broken finger if the kid snatched it this time. From the recesses of his old head he found the music and snatches of words: "Sentimental journey home. Packed my bags, got my reservation."

The kid was still there. "That's nice, mister. You mind if I listen some more?" He sat down uninvited on an adjoining bench that half-faced Marvin, closer but less menacing than standing. He wore khakis and a white shirt, open-collared, maybe a school uniform.

"Sure." As though he had a choice. "It's old-time music, though."

"I know," the kid said. "I have a CD: *The Big Band Era*."

So he tried a few more, "Tuxedo Junction" and "Chattanooga Choo Choo." His lips were sore, but he finished with "Stars and Stripes Forever," John Philip Sousa, with that blazing descending line on the trombone: bam de-bam de-bam de-bam de-bam-bam-bam-bam and into the melody. It was like he'd played it only yesterday.

The kid actually applauded. "So where can I get a mouthpiece?"

"At a music store. I'm not sure you can find one around here anymore. I've got to go along now." That sounded abrupt. He didn't want to sound scared. "What's your name?"

"Elijah, sir. Elijah Williams."

The "sir" was reassuring. "I'm Marvin. Marvin Stein." That was safe enough; the house and telephone were in Max and Dora's names.

"Nice to meet you, Mr. Stein. If I get a mouthpiece, can I try your trombone?"

He didn't want to make promises; Elijah might come back next time with his friends. "Sure. If we happen to meet again." That sounded too brusque. "You can probably get an inexpensive plastic one that's almost as good as the metal."

"Oh, thank you, Mr. Stein. I'll be here tomorrow morning."

"Well, I may be too. No promises, okay?" He took the trombone apart and put it away, aware of Elijah's rapt attention. As he stood, the kid got up too and reached out to offer a handshake that Marvin could hardly avoid. "Thank you, sir. Hope to see you again."

Sure he was being watched as he threaded through the trees, he turned left when he got to the street, and walked all the way around the block before going into the house.

"Hi, Papa." Dora had the baby on her hip. "How did it go? You weren't long."

"The lips are a little tender. It was good. I still know how to play."

"And no one bothered you, right?"

"A teenager came to watch, but he seemed okay. I wondered why he wasn't in school."

"We're on split sessions this year. Overcrowding." Dora was on maternity leave from teaching, and Max taught too. "The state made them close one ancient school as unsafe. Did you get his name?"

"He said Elijah Williams. I walked around the block, coming home, so he wouldn't see where we live."

"Papa, you're too much! I don't remember that name. We'll ask Max tonight."

"No, I don't know him," Max said at dinner. "It's a big city. He sounds okay to me, though. You can't live in fear, papa."

That hurt. Marvin liked to show it was still his neighborhood, so most days he walked six blocks to see if he would make a *minyan* at the storefront temple, but he avoided the other side of the park, and always left his wallet home.

"Why don't you give him a lesson?" Max said.

"Good idea, papa," Dora said. "You could be good for him."

"Be a *mensch*," Max said.

"It could be a *mitzvah*," Dora said.

He wasn't sure. Still, after dinner he went back to the attic and found a few yellowed sheets of beginner's music. He woke next morning determined to give it a try. To be honest, although he loved reading to little Effie, sitting in his lap, he'd wished the new baby would be a grandson.

Elijah was waiting, triumphantly holding up a metal mouthpiece. "The music teacher loaned it to me."

"Good morning, Elijah. Why didn't she lend you the whole trombone?"

"It's ruined, Mr. Stein. In the band bus coming back from a football game, somebody sat on it. A big guy. She said I might as well use the mouthpiece, because nobody's going to use the rest of it ever again."

Marvin put his trombone together. "How did your parents come to name you, Elijah?"

"My mother, sir. My father is . . . not living with us. She sang the hymn, "Elijah won't you blow your horn," with the church choir, and liked the name. I told her about you last night. She likes the idea of me blowing a trombone."

"Playing, Elijah." He had the music stand set up with the beginner's sheet music. "Do you read music?"

"No, sir. I sing in the choir, but I learn by listening. I'd like to read music, though."

"Maybe you should learn that at school. For now, forget the sheet music. Here." He demonstrated how to hold the trombone, the looped horn resting on his shoulder, and showed the slide positions. "You have to play by ear, anyway. No keys; you make the notes with the slide." He took the mouthpiece out. "And with your lips." He held it to his lips and played a scale.

Elijah's eyes widened. "That's neat, Mr. Stein. You don't even need the horn."

A warning light went off in the back of Marvin's head. He didn't need the horn?

He brushed the thought back. "That's just to show that your lips make a difference." He handed Elijah the trombone. "Go ahead, put your mouthpiece in. See if you can make a high note and a low note without moving the slide."

It sounded like a sick foghorn, but Elijah got it. Marvin showed him how to use the slide to make notes all the way up one octave. Then up another register. He had a good ear. Marvin couldn't remember his own first lesson, but Elijah seemed more of a natural than he'd been.

"What was it you were playing yesterday, Mr. Stein?"

" 'Ole Buttermilk Sky.' Hoagy Carmichael." He put his own mouthpiece back in and played it all the way through, then handed the trombone over. "I'll sing it and you play." His voice was as croaky as an old crow, though. He took the trombone back, put in his mouthpiece, played the first passage and handed it back. They went back and forth like that through the whole piece, he cawing the words and playing a few bars, then swapping mouthpieces, Elijah finally playing it all the way through.

The kid really could learn by ear. Marvin applauded.

Elijah grinned and looked embarrassed. "That was fun, Mr. Stein. But I have to get to school soon. Can we do it again?"

A moment's hesitation. But why not? "Of course."

"Tomorrow's Saturday, though. We're Seventh Day Adventists. Could we do it Sunday morning?"

Imagine, they had the same Sabbath. "Sunday morning would be perfect. About ten o'clock?"

"Thank you. I can hardly wait." Elijah put his mouthpiece in his pocket and went off whistling Hoagy's tune.

Sunday dawned a beautiful day. Even though Dora always fixed a big breakfast, they were finished by nine. He should have suggested earlier. He fussed with the newspaper, unable to concentrate. It was still before ten when he set out across the street. Elijah was there.

"Good morning, Mr. Stein. Guess what? The music teacher got me started on reading music, and gave me some to take home. My mother coached me after church yesterday. Did you bring some sheet music?"

Marvin had been refreshing his memory with the brittle old pages, but hadn't seen any point in bringing them. "No. I will tomorrow. Do you want to try a new tune by ear?"

"Absolutely!"

So they did Glenn Miller's "Tuxedo Junction." In half an hour Elijah had not only learned the notes but had the rhythm, too. The park was slow to fill up on a Sunday morning, so they went on to try Tommy Dorsey's "All The Things You Are."

"I think you have real talent, Elijah. Does your mother work, besides singing in the church choir?"

"Oh, yes, sir. She's a para."

Marvin had an idea what paras did in school; Dora and Max talked about them. "A paraprofessional."

"Yes, sir."

"Is she home now?"

"I think so. In fact, she may be peeking out the window, trying to see us."

Through the thin foliage across the great lawn were faded red brick buildings, three-story walk-ups. A good mother might worry whether her son was being hustled by a dirty old man. "I used to have a hardware store over there. It had a lead strip over the doorway with pictures of tools beaten into it."

"I know it exactly!" Elijah said. "That was you?"

"The lead strip is still there?"

"Yes, sir, but it's a cell phone store now. Mama says the

man does drugs on the side; she won't let me go in there."

"How about we walk over there?"

"Now, Mr. Stein?"

"Why not? I'd like to meet your mother. Tell her she's been a good mother and has a talented boy."

Elijah fairly beamed, but then his face clouded. "It's not a very good neighborhood, Mr. Stein."

"I know that. I don't mind."

"On Sunday morning especially. There are men sleeping on the street, hung over or strung out."

"I've seen drunks before, Elijah."

"Maybe you should take the trombone home first, sir. It would be terrible if some druggie snatched it."

"Don't worry. You carry it. Let's go."

glad you're here, dip pen & India ink on paper, by Clare Johnson

Yesterday's Rain

John Olson

I didn't see the rain yesterday. Our blinds were drawn. They're new blinds, not brand new, relatively new, and already broken. Our cat managed to balance herself on the back of the computer desk and swat at the cord and chew the tassel so that it had to be rethreaded. Rethreading, however, did not go as planned. The tassel is dicey. It will endure several gingerly executed pulls, but pull too hard and it comes undone. The easiest solution is to not lift the blinds. This is easily accomplished, as we have no great view, and enjoy our privacy.

Our window is flush with the ground. We overlook dirt, and a few bedraggled plants. I prefer this. I like being partially underground. It gives me a secure feeling. I feel grounded.

I'm not into views. I once lived on the upper floor of an apartment with a panoramic view of Seattle's Lake Union, downtown Seattle, and the east side of Queen Anne Hill. I looked at sailboats, whitecaps on windy days, and the seaplanes from Kenmore Air come and go. It wasn't long before I lost interest. I prefer dirt.

The place where I truly feel at home is in a book. This is where the real panoramas are. The landscapes of the human imagination. Oceans, raging rivers, philosophies, forests. Language is a wilderness and books are their reserves.

If I'm in line at the DMV and I open a book I feel at home. If I'm at the airport, dentist office, hospital waiting room, coffeehouse or bench at the city park and I open a book I feel at home.

Home is a sensation. Shelter, yes. Home is definitely shelter and I love that aspect of it. I say a prayer to the gods of electricity and running water every day. I do not take them for granted. A power outage that lasts more than eight hours is a reminder of how dependent we are on services to give that sheltering aspect of our homes real meaning. It makes me wonder what the hell libertarians are thinking when they squawk about the unnecessary burdens of municipal and federal agencies that ensure clean water and safe roads and standards for electrical wiring and outlets.

That said, home is quintessentially a feeling. The expression "I feel at home here" is indicative of that. I've lived in a lot of places over the years. I've lived in a school bus, hotel, boarding house, and garage. Some places felt naturally good and some places remained cold and unaccepting.

My first home was a human body. A female. My mother. I have absolutely no memory of ever being a zygote, tadpole, or humanoid floating in amniotic fluid. But I spent the first nine months of my existence living like that, rent free. It would be an interesting exercise to figure out at what point in human development a sense of self first begins. It's that sense of self that is our true first home. No sense of self, no home.

Some people are at home in themselves and some people (my tribe) never completely feel at home in themselves. There's always something inside agitating, churning, ruminating, preventing me from that idyllic sense of being comfortable in one's own skin. Sometimes a good feeling comes along and I will feel completely at home in my body, muscles relaxed, brain relaxed, my nerves flickering like little scented votive candles in a quiet Mexican church. It can be encouraged. It can be enhanced with a little wine, a little Vicodin, a little Xanax. Meditation helps, as does exercise. That boil inside can be brought down to a nice little bubbly simmer. Feelings can be mellowed. Attitudes can be softened.

Votive candles lit, confessions made, prayers recited.

The *Agenbite of Inwyt*, subtitled Remorse (*Prick) of Conscience,* is a confessional prose work written in Middle English by a Benedictine monk named Michael of Northgate sometime in the thirteenth century. The work did not garner a large and enduring audience but is most notable because

James Joyce borrowed the title for referencing states of inner agitation and pain in *Ulysses.*

Remorse is awful. I hate remorse. I never cease obsessing about building a time machine and going back to edit my life, undo all the horrendous mistakes made, horrible things said, wrong turns made, opportunities lost, bad choices made. People always say "let go." You can't go back, you can't do anything, so what's the point of dwelling on it? None, obviously. I get that. I'm on board with that. I would love to let go. But how do you let go of a feeling? It's not a rope, not a wing strut, not a bowling ball. The hand has no purchase on it. It's a feeling. It doesn't have a shape, a texture, a knob or a handle. There are no levers or buttons. It's not like an elevator. I can't make it go up or down. I can't steer it. Feelings are ghosts. They're phantasmal. When we're troubled with remorse we say we are haunted by something. The mind is preoccupied, and the tenant is a shapeless, formless apparition.

Specter, shadow, wraith.

Anxiety isn't much fun either. That chronic sense of dread, of things going horribly wrong at any minute. Anxiety is a form of fear; what makes it different from fear is its irrationality, its presumption of harm where there may be no harm, its exaggeration of something scary that might not be all that bad. We just don't know. It's the uncertainty that drives us nuts. It's a fear of something that might happen, not (as for example being chased by a bear) something that is actually happening.

Psychologists give that inner discomfort a nifty little term: fight or flight. But fight what? Flee from what? If we knew the answer to that, we would be instantly relieved. We would be more at home in our bodies. We would know what to do. Resignation isn't such a bad thing either. If there's nothing we can do, if hope is more painful than helpful, surrender to a helpless situation can be liberating. It frees us from responsibility. We play a sonata on the violin while the Titanic sinks.

Or we can seek therapy. A skilled psychologist can help us to see the irrationality of a fear. The ghost will vanish. Though, as in the recent election, some fears aren't so irrational. Sometimes the things we dread do come to life. Godzilla rises from the New York harbor and starts crushing cars and buildings. A moronic fascist billionaire is elected president and critical social services are destroyed and people die.

Mortality doesn't help. Knowing one is going to die one day isn't conducive to a homey feeling inside oneself. The ship is going down. You really get that message when you turn sixty. By the time you turn seventy you're almost giddy with impermanence. Upkeep? There's no remodeling for the temple that is the body. This is where you learn stoicism.

Stoicism is a home for pessimists. Or should I say realists? Let's say realists.

Stoicism is a home for realists. The Stoics believed that we can become immune to misfortune if we cultivate certain virtues, such as developing the intellect and creating a philosophical perspective on life. But what does that mean, "philosophical perspective?" It means tapping into the idea of the universe and all beings and matter within the universe as being unified by breath, by pneuma, by Godstuff. Pneuma is breath and spirit. It is, in many ways, similar to the mindfulness movement. We minimize our pain by concentrating on our breath. By breathing in and breathing out. Our ultimate home may be breathing. Inhaling, exhaling. Letting thoughts pass through our minds like clouds. Let go let God, as they say in AA.

Logic worked for the Stoics but it doesn't always work for me. I do what I can to cultivate a philosophical perspective. Sometimes I succeed, sometimes I fall on my face. Sometimes I just thrash about like a madman, or brood like Hamlet on ghosts and revenge. I seek philosophy. I look for it wherever I can. But it helps considerably to be at home when I undertake that voyage.

Moving Between Houses, Between Countries

Linda Packard

when she squints
it's a film running backwards

she can almost see objects
fly into the distance

down come the Vermeer prints
rolling up as they float to the carpet

books & maps neatly pack themselves
into stiff cardboard boxes

while the desk disassembles itself
the driverless car rolls into storage

words lift from scattered pages
crowd back into cerebral convolutions

in limbo
the world is home

she's all pink new skin
a bathtub Venus rising from saltless water

Late Afternoon Light, photo by Jenn Powers

The Library Study

Sue Gale Pace

The purpose behind interviewing the homeless, as far as Jayne could tell, was to decide how to make the library viable for everyone. Some patrons objected to allowing the homeless inside. Others were all for it. The head librarian was trying to keep the board of directors happy. The board wanted to please the city council. The patrons wanted to check out books, DVDs, and CDs, and the homeless were simply trying to survive.

At the front end of the third floor, by the elevators and restrooms, there were computers where anyone could check their email, help their teenager with a social studies report, or research whatever the heck was making that thumping noise whenever their car turned to the left. The woman behind the desk was tall and imposing with a voice like a bullhorn. She looked the same age as Jayne but dressed like a teenaged Bitch Queen of Darkness with a black leather skirt and a neckline that showed her boob tats. One was a spider and the other one was a fly.

Jayne handed her the letter from the Library Board of Directors. It was cosigned by the mayor. The woman behind the desk read it, frowned, and folded her arms. "Homeless people should have someplace to stay during the day," she said. "They need a place where they can take a crap, wash their hair, brush their teeth, and not be picked on."

"Perfect," Jayne said. "Those are the folks I want to interview. Are there some, uh, regulars?"

"Oh yeah, we got over a hundred singles and about forty families, mostly Moms and kids but sometimes a Dad will show up."

Jayne found it difficult to not stare at the woman's boob tats. "Where would you like me to sit?"

Are you going to be asking really private questions?'

"Yes."

"Then I can put you in an empty study room. It gets stuffy in there but nobody's signed up for it."

"Thank you."

"How long are you going to need it?"

"Until Saturday."

"Whoa! I thought you meant for a couple hours tonight."

"For tonight," Jayne said slowly, "and until the project ends, on Saturday."

"What kind of questions will you be asking?"

"Lifestyle questions."

"Give me some examples."

Jayne knew that "lifestyle" was one of those words that carried a thousand meanings including fun, horrid, and boring. In this study, she assumed horrid would lead the pack. She flipped through a questionnaire packet and read a sample from each page. "Where do you get your clothes? Where do you sleep at night? How often do you use the food bank or the free kitchen or dumpsters? Have you ever sold drugs? Have you ever been arrested?" Jayne stuffed the paper packets back in the canvas bag. "Things like that."

"People actually answer those questions?"

"Yes. Amazing isn't it." Jayne smiled. "Of course I give them an incentive."

"What's that mean?"

"I give them money."

"How much?"

"I make it worth their time. And it's in cash."

"You aren't going to ask names and birthdates and social security numbers and shit like that?"

"No." Jayne resisted looking at her watch. "I'll ask about race and education and job history. Mostly I'll ask what the library does for them that they can't get anywhere else."

"They get me!" the reference librarian boomed. "I don't let anyone mess with them!"

Jayne put down the canvas bag that held her supplies, smiled and held out her hand. "I'm Jayne Corwin," she said. "I'm so happy to be working with you."

"I'm Rita." The Bitch Queen of Darkness didn't take Jayne's offer of a handshake. Her frown was appraising. "If I learn that you're scamming these people, you'll be dealing with the Goddess of the Reference Desk."

Jayne lowered her outstretched hand. "Is that what you call yourself?"

"No, she's my supervisor and she makes me look like Hello Kitty."

"As the letter stated," Jayne kept her voice neutral, "the Head Librarian and Mayor Benson want me here."

Rita's frown deepened but she handed Jayne the key to the study room.

Once inside the glass-windowed room, Jayne took out a packet of questionnaires, rearranged the chairs around the table, and stowed her purse under the table. She had been working local surveys for a couple of years but the money was barely enough to make the payments on her condo. Dolly, her supervisor, wanted Jayne to work fulltime as a traveling field interviewer but the thought of driving all over the United States, in a beater Honda, frightened Jayne.

"I really think you're ready to move ahead in the company," Dolly had said, but Jayne's silence was answer enough. Dolly sighed, "just know there's a fulltime job waiting for you."

The next few hours went quickly. Rita directed panhandlers and street teens Jayne's way. About an hour before the library closed, Rita brought in a sad little family. The leader of the pack seemed to be a teenaged mother of two, plus her older disabled sister, and their mother.

Nobody said anything while Jane explained she would ask questions and mark their responses for them.

"How long is this going to take?" the teenager asked.

"Not long," Jayne said. "How much time do you spend in the library?"

"We're here all the time." The girl was burping the baby. The toddler was gnawing on a granola bar.

"From opening to closing," her mother said. "We've got an old Toyota pickup we're living in. We got a camper shell." The older woman looked to be in her fifties though it was hard to judge what with the worry lines and no makeup. "It gets crowded during the day so the library's just the ticket."

"Finding a place to park is a fulltime job," the teenager said. "If it stays in one place too long we'll get a ticket. And I got to be gone a lot of the day because I got a corner on Pike and Second. The dealers let me panhandle if I give them a cut."

The older woman lifted a toddler onto her lap. "They got story time for kids here and the children's librarian sneaks us soap and shampoo if we ask nice."

"I wash," the disabled sister said. There was a horrible scar circling her forehead and one eye wandered fiercely. Jayne thought it could have been a car wreck or possibly an abusive partner. "I pee," the sister said. "You pretty. I like you."

The mother wiped spittle from the older girl's mouth. "I watch the kids while Marilee and Sis are busy. I don't like her takin' the little kids to panhandle."

"We'd get more, if we did." Marilee picked up the sign she'd made using the standard black permanent marker on cardboard. *Homeless. Please Help*. On the back it said. *God Bless You*. "We're wasting time here."

"I'm interviewing homeless people who use the library," Jayne said. "We have some incentive money to thank respondents for their time."

"How much?" the teenager asked. "And do we all get paid or just Ma?"

"Everyone I interview gets paid."

"Even the kids?"

"I don't interview anyone under eighteen."

"How come?" Marilee folded her thin arms. "Lots of homeless moms are under eighteen."

"I don't actually ask to see a birth certificate or anything," Jayne said. "I just ask how old you are. Are you over eighteen?"

"Sure."

Jane kept her face smooth. "We pay $30 for a twenty-minute interview."

"And Ma and me and Sis would each get $30?"

"Yes." Jayne read them the statement of confidentiality.

"That means no matter what I say you can't tell on us." The younger girl's face still held a frown.

"Right," Jayne said.

"Ask away."

The baby started to cry so the older woman took everyone else from the room and sat outside playing Patty Cake and singing softly.

"It helps me to keep things clear if I have names," Jayne said. "No last names or birthdates—just what you go by." Jayne tried for perky. "You can give me an initial if you want. You could be A. Your mother could be B. Your sister could be. . . ."

"I'm Marilee."

"Why aren't you taking welfare?"

"We're kinda keeping under the radar."

"Because?"

"Because I don't want to go to juvie and leave my Ma and Sis and the kids."

"Felony or misdemeanor?"

"I stole some stuff from the store. Tampax and formula and shit like that. When the cops were talking to the manager, I took off. I don't actually know what the charges are but it's not the first time I took what we needed so I know I'll be inside for a while."

"Why are you living in a pickup?"

"We got kicked out of one place already so we got no references."

"Why did you get kicked out?"

"Alex crapped all over the carpet and he'd bark every time somebody walked past our door."

"Alex? Barked?"

"Yeah, he's a Beagle and they do that. Protecting their pack."

Jayne was flipping pages and finding questions pertaining to households and scribbling in responses as fast as she could. "So the dog's name is Alex," she said. "Any other pets?"

"Nope."

"Isn't it expensive to feed a dog?"

"Yeah."

"Why keep him?"

"Because he tells us when Sis is going to have a seizure."

"Does Sis get a disability check?"

"Yeah, but we haven't got it for a couple months now. When we got kicked out of our apartment the disability check didn't have no place to go." The girl's shoulders were tight, humped up around her neck like two knots of worry, and she stared at Jayne, daring her to disagree. "It costs money to get a Post Office Box plus they got rules and shit and I'm afraid they could trace where we are."

Sitting across from Jayne, Marilee looked about twelve. Her shoulders were still tight but the hostile gaze had shifted to something resembling despair. Her jeans were dirty and so was her tee shirt. It had a faded Mariners logo. There weren't any track marks on her arms and her eyes were neither dilated nor had they shrunk to pin pricks. No drugs, Jayne thought, and she marked another box in the interview packet.

Jayne asked the girl questions about support systems and education and lifestyle and health. She asked about family and friends. She asked about resources and income and hopes for the future.

Most of the girl's answers were negative. They didn't have anything.

"What would you like the library to have?"

"Besides a shower and free lunch?"

Jayne smiled. "Yes, besides that."

"I'd like to get my GED." The girl scratched her tangled hair. "That Goth reference lady said I could maybe do that online but we need the money I make and I can't leave Sis and Ma on my corner. Ma gets kinda spooked out there plus she's right, it's too hard on the little kids."

"How old are they?"

"One and three."

Jayne put down her pen. "They're your sister's?"

"The state wants to take them from us," the girl said. "They said she's too disabled to take care of them plus we don't got no place to keep 'em."

"Do you have any family who can help you out?"

Her answer was sharp. "No!"

"Friends?"

"I already told you, we got no one." The girl grabbed Jayne's wrist. "You can't tell anyone where the kids are."

Jayne nodded. "No, I can't. It's illegal for me to tell on you. They could fine me $50,000—which I don't have—and they could send me to jail for a year." All of which was true.

"Okay," The girl said.

Jayne turned the page to the next set of questions. When Merilee was finished, Ma came in. Jayne asked her the same questions and got the same negative answers. When Sis sat at the table she answered what she could, mostly keeping her eyes down and shrugging. At the end she looked at Jayne with the most beautiful clear blue eyes and said, "I like books with pictures." Jayne left most of the questions blank, counted out $90, plus a ten from her own practically empty wallet, and asked Ma what they'd do with the incentive money. Jayne was thinking a night in a motel. Shoes. A real meal someplace. But Ma had a different idea.

"We'll have to get tabs for the pickup," the woman said. "That'll take most of it. If there's anything left over I'm gonna hide it away. I'm trying to save enough to get Marilee some of those glasses they got over at Walgreen Drugs. That girl can't see which is why she can't pass the GED."

That night Jayne Corwin went home to the condo to sleep in her own bed and felt guilty about being warm and clean and fed. She wished she could pour all the money she had down the rat hole of that little family's life. But if she did that, Jayne would also be the one who was homeless.

By the end of the second day, it became clear that the majority of people Jayne would interview were male and single and obviously needed what the library had already been providing for years; a safe place to sleep. One man was a Vietnam Vet missing an arm and a leg. There were a couple of Desert Storm Vets and also some young guys, fresh back from the war with head scars and desert camo. A few of the others were neat and clean but most wore multiple sets of coats and pants and had the ripe smell of dead fish. There were dozens of them and they hid away in various corners, sometimes slumped in a chair, stinking of alcohol but mostly smelling of despair and loss and bewilderment. "I used to be a person," one man said to her. "How the hell did this happen to me?"

The street teens came in the afternoons. They bristled with metal face studs and tats and impatience. Mostly they used the bathrooms, talked animatedly, and eyed the bag where Jayne kept the incentive money.

"Rita knows where I am and what I'm doing," she told everyone she interviewed. "She'll kick you out of the library if you screw with me."

They all understood that. This was Rita's floor. She may have looked and sounded like a Bitch Queen of Darkness but she worked like the Nun of Divine Intervention. She answered the telephone, connected the computers, helped the patrons locate whatever it was they needed, and took care of the homeless. The person who was supposed to be in charge, the disheveled and constantly frowning Reference Librarian, crabbed at everyone, including the janitor, the security guard, and even Jayne Corwin. Fortunately, she usually stayed in her office and swore at her computer.

Ma wasn't lying when she said her family spent all of its time in the library. She and the two youngest spent hours in the children's section, one floor down. Jayne would see them when she went for lunch. Ma read to the little ones constantly or drew pictures of puppies and kittens on the back of scraps of paper she'd found. Jayne found one of those scraps and bent to put it in the recycling box but couldn't because of the perfection of pointed ears and fluffy paws. Ma had talent but she also had arthritis and her gnarled fingers had trouble holding onto the stubby pencils she pilfered from the library's computer area. Nevertheless, Ma hugged the little ones and changed stinky diapers and taught them Patty Cake and Peek-a-boo. The money from Sis's and Marilee's panhandling paid for those diapers and for formula and burgers and dog food. It also paid for Sis's seizure medication. There wasn't anything left after that.

By the third day, word got around—answer some easy questions and you get some easy money. Other women started to show up. There were plenty of hard luck stories —of dreams shot down and blindsided hopes. Some of the women were hookers on break, and some were addicts who came to the library because there was shade in the summer and warmth in the winter. Some brought children but most didn't. The kids were in school, in foster care, at a friend's, or with relatives. Rita weeded out the ones who were there on a lark along with the ones who never visited the library, even in the worst of times, but thought answering a few questions would be an easy way to score. The library study wasn't about them. It was about the people who came, day in and day out, and pretended to read in order to feel safe for a few hours.

Jayne and Rita had taken to having lunch together at the little coffee shop across the street from the library. Jayne mentioned her husband walking out, leaving her with an outrageous mortgage and a crummy car. Rita talked about school loans and low wages.

"Are you going to finish those chips?" Rita asked.

Jayne handed over the small unopened bag and watched Rita put it into her purse. "I thought you were going to eat them," Jayne said.

"I'll give them to Ma so that Marilee and Sis can have a little treat when they come back."

Jayne didn't say what was on her mind, that Ma and her family should be eating real food and not chips or ninety-nine cent hamburgers every night. But there was no kitchen, no pots and pans, no oven. Even macaroni and cheese was out of the question. Fresh fruits and veggies cost an arm and a leg. Soup would have to be eaten cold from the can. Jayne went to the counter and bought what was left of the red apples and ripe bananas in a basket by the cash register. She handed them to Rita. "I hate this study."

"It just shows how fucked up the system really is." Rita stood, all six foot, two inches of her, and brushed crumbs from her chest and lap. "I'm living with my parents but I could easily be one of the homeless."

"That's why you protect them."

Rita looked at the far wall and nodded. "I don't like living with my folks, and they aren't happy about having me on the living room couch, but we've adapted."

Jayne said nothing. After her husband left, Jayne hadn't adapted to life after her divorce. She had walked away from a good job and moved into a one bedroom condo. She hadn't answered texts or Facebook inquiries from friends, work-mates, and school chums to have coffee or lunch. She hadn't adapted to what it took to maintain any of it. It was why she, Jayne Corwin, was asking questions for the census, Public

Health, The Department of Labor, and the Library Board. She was afraid to start over.

But adapting was tweaking your life, she thought. Push a little this way and prod a lot that way. It was making your life work for you.

"We should have dinner this weekend," Rita said. "There's a great place downtown that serves this Moroccan chicken and date combination. It's to die for."

"Maybe," Jayne said. She watched Rita head out the door and stride up the block toward the library. People moved out of her way but some homeless men, clustered by the fire hydrant across the street, lifted their heads and barely moved their fingers to say, "Hey, friend." Rita never hailed them back but gave a quick jutting of the chin before she charged on. It was nice to watch, Jayne thought. Those small gestures of acknowledgement brought sudden tears to her eyes.

Saturday came and Jayne stowed two packed suitcases and not much else into her car. The day was crammed with interviews and suddenly Rita was closing up—switching off the computers and the lights and shaking awake the security guard so he could wander the stacks, herding the patrons and homeless toward the Exits.

"Want to go for a drink?"

Jayne shook her head.

Rita stared down at her. "We could be friends," she said.

"I agree." Jayne shouldered her computer and took out the bright red umbrella Dolly had given her at the last training.

"Will you at least come and have lunch with me sometimes?"

It was an opportunity to begin again, Jayne thought. Humans do that, they build little communities. They help each other. They forge connections. It's the best part of being human, Jayne thought, and I've refused to do that. She and Rita, bundled in beaded raincoats, stood at the top of the steps, looking down as the stragglers wandered into a cold spring rain. Ma was carrying the sleeping baby and Sis had the toddler by the hand. Marilee had the greasy bag of burgers in one hand and Alex's rope leash in the other. "Absolutely," she said. "but not right away."

A wind had kicked up and as the family stood at the curb, waiting for the light to change, a car drove past. The splash from the puddle drenched them but they didn't seem to notice. They were anxious to get back to their pickup and to food and to a dreamless sleep.

Jayne thought of her condo; there were dishes there and glasses and an oven and refrigerator. There was safety. There were rules against pets but maybe Alex could live in the back of the pickup until they got settled and got the disability check and maybe some welfare and food stamps and eyeglasses.

Jayne handed Rita the keys; one was for the condo's locked downstairs door and one for her unit. "I'm going away for a while and I don't want to leave my place empty. You could live there . . . or they could. Your choice."

"You've got to be kidding."

Jayne fiddled with her umbrella and shook her head. "Everything is included; heat, lights, insurance. I'm signing up for a new study and I'll be working out of town for six months."

"So you'd let them have it if I stayed at my folks?"

"I trust you," Jayne said softly. "You decide . . . but somebody has to live there."

"You can't change your mind." Rita was suddenly fierce. "I'd testify in court that you wanted it to be this way."

"It's temporary," Jayne said. "Six months or so and then I'll have to get it back."

"Okay," Rita said. "I could testify to that."

"We're not frigging going to need to go to court!" Jayne said. "It's just that I don't need my condo right now. I will later. But for right now it's silly to have it sit empty."

The rain began again and Jayne's umbrella bloomed like an inverted peony, red and full.

Rita dodged under the umbrella's canopy to hug her. "You're a good woman," Rita whispered, "and they need it more than I do. Don't worry, I'll check on them, sometimes." Keys jangling, she scrambled down the wet steps to catch up to the little family.

Jayne headed the other direction. The streetlights were on and she stepped quickly through intermittent pools of light, making her way to the parking lot. She couldn't decide if she was walking away from her old life or returning to an updated, better version of it. She would spend six months living in southern motels, eating at various fast food joints and skyping with . . . she paused to think who would want to hear from her. Skyping with Rita, she decided, and maybe that was enough to get the adaptation ball rolling.

Jayne climbed into her ancient Honda and turned the key. The engine started up quickly and purred like a contented kitten. If she believed in omens, which she steadfastly didn't, she would think things were getting off to a good start.

late February, dip pen & India ink on paper, by Clare Johnson

At One Time or Another

Taurus Moon Dream

Linda Packard

Haven't we all dreamed
of finding locked doors
in our own houses
ones we've never seen before?

Haven't we miraculously moved
through those doors into spacious
rooms, one after the other
each more fantastic than the last?

And who hasn't dreamed
of finding an open coffin
framed by a window in a room
crowded with overstuffed furniture?

Or maybe you've turned a corner,
into a garden stretching to the horizon,
where a golden sarcophagus
fills an open grave with wild light?

How cool!

Robert Ronnow

How cool!
this early summer evening
after a day so oppressive
even we New Yorkers move painstakingly.
The breeze in sumac trees
so why am I not more content?
The electricity went off at the bank,
spontaneous bank holiday,
so I'm broke, drinking water.

All my needs except love
fulfilled. Woman
opens her windows. How cool!
this summer evening
in New York, dense New York
the jets overhead
the people on the ground suffering
and struggling toward vague goals
or goals clear as Harry Helmsley's.

How cool and refreshing
this glass of ice water
after today's hot pavement, clothes.
During the afternoon heat
I sleep in my underwear.
What a city I murmur to myself
looking at its map. Big,
Jamaica Bay to Inwood,
the Battery to Pelham Bay.

Nowadays novels need
a few cities to move the plot.
New York, Saigon, Paris.
The protagonist
does not walk in the park. He
uses his car to get around fast.
How cool this evening in New York!
Lost among the bars and industry,
moonrise over Bronx.

Exile

Judith Skillman

Four apples in a bowl.
Thick inch of blue half circling,
and the stem of one rising
like a Byzantine Church.
Where will we go when the shadows
leave the fruit? Four apples
in a row. Each casting
its own elongated oval
charged with purples, greens, blues.
How will we know what to do
when the sadness comes?
Even the broken eggs, half-shells
done in yellow white,
lie stiffly as bird beaks
with no song.

The Camphor Harem

Michael Philips

Six East lay at the southern edge of the hospital. A high concrete wall set it apart from the always-congested road, and a gate of rusted steel stood between it and Six West, the psychiatric jail.

There was a camphor tree at the gate, its bark wizened and scaly, home to kingdoms of brown ants and a nomad scorpion or two. The leaves smelled perfect, and in winter Six East's nurses boiled them on an old rocket stove to perfume the ward; hence the ward's sassy nickname, the Camphor Harem.

Dr Ahmed Biomy clanged the bell at the gate and waited. He'd finished his overnight shift at the jail over an hour ago, but had put off this visit till he'd smoked four cigarettes and guzzled two mugs of tea. Of all his morning rounds, this was the most painful. He'd rather have bribed a colleague to come in his stead, but unfortunately that no longer was possible.

Soon a nurse came lurching toward him, wrapping a white scarf round her head. "I'll let you in in a sec, Doctor," she said softly, unlocking the gate.

"Is Miss Fatima in yet?" he asked. "I haven't seen you before."

"Her daughter's *henna* is tonight," the nurse said. "She's off for a week." The nurse allowed him in then relocked the gate, gurgling deeply in her throat, and spat on the dust.

She's sick, the young doctor realized morosely. *I thought she was being friendly.*

They walked together past the camphor tree, to the sunbleached green building of the ward. "The patients were unbelievable," the nurse said. "They kept me up all night. Doctors go to bed, and we nurses don't have a moment of rest."

"I was right next to you at the jail all night," Ahmed said. "Why didn't you call for me or the resident on duty?"

"I can't talk now, Doctor. My voice is gone." She mounted the four concrete steps leading up to a chipped white door. "You know your way around. Call for me if you need me." And she vanished into the ward.

Ahmed stood there for a moment, the winter sun feeling harsher than usual on his fair skin, and he replayed their brief conversation in his head, befuddled by a mix of lack of sleep and nicotine and caffeine. *Did she mention her name?* he thought. He soon gave up and pushed himself up the steps and into the belly of the ward.

The ward had a simple structure. Two eight-bed rooms, one washroom, a large hall for eating and other daily activities, and a small office near the door. All Ahmed had to do was to take two wide side steps to the right, and he'd lock himself up in his office all morning. There, he would renew the treatment plans of all the patients without seeing a single one of them, which he'd been doing for weeks anyway.

In fact, Miss Fatima, the absent chief nurse, was herself his biggest ally in maintaining this ignoble routine. It seemed far-fetched now, but when he'd recently been assigned to the ward, the pretty chief nurse had been very nice to him. She smiled, told him she had a single daughter six years younger than himself (who'd finished an accounting degree and had turned down dozens of offers from merchants, tradesmen, and even lawyers, because she wanted a doctor); she patted him on the elbow, and giggled with her grand bosom bouncing up and down; she told him all his jokes were very funny.

But their honeymoon rapidly slipped into a bog of disenchantment, and then it was all over. It had started when Dr Ahmed had mixed up the treatment plans of two chronic patients, a schizophrenic called Zeinab with a manic-depressive called Hanaa. That could have passed, had it not been followed by Miss Fatima's pharyngitis, which the great Dr Ahmed failed to prescribe an effective antibiotic for and was later laughed at by the real doctor the chief nurse went to see.

Ahmed's image crumbled for all the right reasons. A wrong dose here, missed diagnosis there, and absurd patient record-taking in-between. Soon he was out of grace, a laughing stock. The Camphor Harem, not without sympathy, had come to the sad conclusion Dr Ahmed Biomy was no real doctor. His mind, and heart, lay elsewhere. He, therefore, needed to not see too much of the patients.

Emboldened by the chief nurse's absence, though, Ahmed Biomy briskly broke into restricted territory; he went to the hall. Astonishingly, no one was there. A table was missing, but the other—oblong, covered with blue damask—carried the remnants of today's breakfast: *fino* bread, strawberry jam, *La Vache Qui Ri* triangles, and white plastic cups to receive tea from a giant teapot perched over a copper tray on a chair. The rocket stove was actively boiling with the camphor leaves sending off the heady aroma, but it made it difficult for him to discern the cacophony of sounds echoing around.

He walked about, cocked his ears, and it was unmistakable. Giggles bursted out off the far room, interspersed by chatter.

"Miss! Miss!" he cried. "Where are you? Miss!"

In a moment Miss Lubna, one of the nurses he knew by name, came out of the room. "Yes, Doctor."

"Where's everybody?" he asked. "The patients should be taking their showers by now." "They've already taken their showers, Doctor," Miss Lubna said, smiling. "Go to your office, Doctor. I'll be there in five."

"What's going on, Miss?"

"Nothing is going on, Doctor."

"How come nothing is going on? I hear laughs and noise from that room. What're you up to?"

"Oh, you're asking about that?" The nurse said carefully, drawling her words and nodding with her whole body. "It's the Christmas."

"The Christmas?"

"The Christmas, Doctor. The New Year thing? We're decorating the rooms for the patients."

"Get me a patient in my office right now, Miss," Ahmed snapped. "I'll be writing a memo in five minutes. Understood?"

"Yes, Doctor."

"Five minutes, no more."

He returned to his office, and in less than a minute he'd got his coveted patient. A schizophrenic called Manal, one of the hospital's most loyal clients: been there over twenty times before.

"Olives are many," Manal said, sitting down. The fuchsia scarf she pulled tightly down to her brows lent her cheeks a palish hue. Her hirsute jowls looked tumorous, and her green eyes were restless: two knobs of gum spat onto an engine rocking constantly inside her head. She attempted a futile bite at her trembling fingernails.

"I'm the doctor, Manal," Ahmed said with a forced smile. "Do you remember me?"

"The cow. Here? Darwish and his wife . . . hmm."

"Darwish and his wife," Ahmed echoed her. "What did they say, Manal? Are they your new imaginary friends?" He jerked her file open. Gradually his face turned the color of her scarf.

My fingerprints are all over this crime.

It was he who'd admitted her two months ago; he who'd filled out her scandalous family and past history sheets; and he who'd prescribed her medication: ludicrously cumbersome doses of clozapine, Valium, and a depot Modecate ampoule twice a month. No Cogentin there for the extrapyramidal tremors. No follow-ups since admission.

What had taken possession of me?

He knew her well and knew her family too. He'd seen her off himself to her brother-in- law's car eight months ago, last time she'd been here, back when he was a new resident at the hospital and more invested in his job.

Acting had been but a fantasy then. He'd aspired to be an actor since a very early age, but life simply hadn't taken him in that direction. Then it suddenly came true, and with it all his pretexts for self-deceit dissipated. He saw into himself and knew his heart beat on, and only on, stage. No matter how small his part was, at the National Theater of Attaba he was real. Everywhere else, he acted, and very badly at that.

Poor Manal. How could he ever forget Haldol was her famous elixir, the only antipsychotic she'd responded to of all the fancy replacements the hospital's top psychiatrists had tried to fit on her? *That's ABC psychiatry in this place,* he chastised himself. *Oh, God. Oh, God.*

"The cheese rotted . . . ekhkhkhkh," Manal said.

He closed her file and drummed his fingers on the desk. Through the barred window up behind him sunlight reached down onto his irritable hand. He reached forward and pivoted his chin on his fist, smiling at his victim.

"How's Christmas and sunshine for a match?" he said. "Papa Noelle on the beach. Or a camphor Christmas tree. Hey, how about A Christmas Carol? I can't imagine a ghost in sunlight, can you, Manal? I've been the Ghost of Christmas Past myself. You know what, I'll show you."

In a surge of energy, the actor sprang off his seat and frolicked forward. He stooped over her and placed his forefinger on her lips. "Your lip is trembling," he said. "And what is that upon your cheek?"

He drew his lips closer to her face, taking in her dancing pupils and blushing face, the scent of soap and the stench of her teeth. The moment he laid his lips on the corner of her mouth, a gong rang out. Then another. And another.

"I thought I'd save you, Manal," he whispered to her. "But it turns out I'm not your hero." He hurried off to the hall.

"Zeinab, you fat-assed cow, you've made it worse!"

"Step away!"

"You leave it to me, Miss Alyaa. I've done it before."

"Done what, Hanaa? It's you who got it stuck to begin with."

"Yoooh!"

Boom. Boom. Boom.

What a beautiful scene!

The patients and the three nurses were all huddled up in one knot. They locked legs, arms, and necks in a strained effort to deliver the steel table missing from the hall through the door.

"Abeer and Hanaa," the nurse who'd let him in said, "you push it on your side, and we'll push from here."

"It won't do, Miss Alyaa," Hanaa, the bipolar whose treatment Ahmed had switched before, said. "The legs'll get stuck."

"Do as I say! Abeer, over here with me, for God's sake."

Miss Abeer, the youngest of the three nurses, hunkered down and joined Miss Alyaa and Miss Lubna on their side of the doorjamb, where the table slanted down. The thing stuck fast, high on the other side of the jamb on its flank, and it did have wide flanks between the legs welded under the edges, a solid mass of steel weighing—much like the one in the hall—over two hundred kilograms. Two thirds of it were in, and one out.

An elderly patient whose name Ahmed forgot crawled underneath the table, emerged on the other side, and pulled in the hall's direction. The women inside pushed in the same direction. The table tore against the jamb and rushed to the hall, punching the elderly woman to the floor. She fell on her back. Then the two hind legs of the table hit the jamb and balked and one of the front legs banged on the floor near the woman's head.

Ahmed finally walked over. He saw the blue, red, and yellow balloons and the garish decorations on the ceiling inside the room. The three nurses had abandoned the impossible task, snagged as it was, and were checking for injuries.

Some patients were clambering under the table to get out.

"This is dangerous," Ahmed said. "I've been in my office all along. I don't bite."

Miss Alyaa flicked her wrist in his direction dismissively. "Thank you."

"Go back to your office, Doctor," Miss Abeer said, examining a gnash in Miss Lubna's hand.

"I told you it'd get stuck," Hanaa said to the nurses, standing by his side, picking her panties.

"We need to get this thing out of the way, Hanaa," Ahmed said. He clutched the high legs with his hands. "Everyone, lend me a hand. How did you get it in in the first place?"

"No, no, Doctor," Miss Alyaa cried.

"It should be easier if we flipped it on one side," Ahmed said. He tried to raise it up, but the flank wouldn't budge. "Ladies, here with me."

"The doctor has gone mad." Miss Abeer laughed.

"I've been working in this madhouse for too long, it seems," Ahmed said.

Miss Abeer laughed, and so did some of the patients helping him out. Miss Alyaa smiled and said, "Dr Ahmed," and slapped the back of her wrist.

He was now motivated and he shoved again, without success. "All of you," he yelled to the nurses inside. "I'm big but no Hercules. Come on over."

"All right!" Miss Abeer said.

"My mother-in-law once lifted a whole wagon all by herself," Miss Alyaa said, pounding on the side slanting down. "But her son would've been under the wheels if she hadn't, that's why."

"People in the good old days used to eat well," Miss Abeer said, carefully lowering herself under the high side. When she'd come out on his side her hand brushed against his on the steel flank.

"We're not working together," he groaned. "On my word, one, two, three, and we push up and you push down.

Understood?"

"Zeinab! Pull away your leg; it'll fall on your toes."

"Go ahead, Doctor. I can feel it giving way."

"Ahem. One, two, three!"

Their hands in sync, their elbows locked and their bodies pushed on and away from the table. The high flank inched up at last, then the whole thing dislodged and fell sideways on the floor with a loud thud.

Hanaa said, "Sweet!"

And the others shrieked and leapt, celebrating their victory.

Miss Alyaa ululated and got them in stitches. "I haven't ululated since I gave birth to Mazin."

"Ha ha. It sure felt like labor. How old is Mazin now?"

"My heart drops into my feet when I hear about labor," Miss Lubna said.

"Ladies," Ahmed said, panting and hunching over the thing lying on its side, "this isn't over yet."

They dragged the table around to get the hind legs out. Then they cheered, "Ally-oop!" and strained until they'd heaved it back up on its straight legs.

They whooped, and Miss Alyaa patted him on the back. "By the Prophet you're a hero!"

"I've got to go back to my office, Miss Alyaa," he said.

When he came back next morning, the hall's walls were festooned with all colors of tapestry, a plastic Christmas tree with cotton spun around it stood where the stove used to be, and Miss Lubna was sitting on a chair knitting pink baby socks with her bandaged hand.

"Good morning, Miss Lubna," he said. "How's everything?"

"All is good, Doctor," she said. "We have two new patients. I'll bring them over once they've eaten their breakfast."

"Was someone discharged yesterday? We already have fifteen beds occupied, Miss Lubna."

"Only fourteen, Doctor."

"What's happened to the fifteenth?"

"Manal, she's no longer with us."

"Why, did her sister come to take her home?"

"No, Doctor," the nurse said. "Poor soul. She choked on her dinner last night. We cried our eyes out over her. It's bad for the baby, I know, is it not, Doctor? Would you mind passing me the scissors? Tut. It's scary what an olive pit could do. Relax in your office, Doctor. It's going to take a while; breakfast has just been served."

Gray House on the Corner, Surrounded by Rock Garden,
charcoal sketch by Rebecca Pyle

Upstate

Alison Stone

Redolent of Lysol and cranberry candles, our kitchen
makes me miss Manhattan's rotting trash.
Though the water-logged air makes subterfuge impossible,
we suburbanites try anyway, prime our punch lines,
practice smiling through both sides of our mouths. Coo
over bruise-colored pansies mottling exhausted lawns.
Next year at this time, we'll be in the same spot
as if frozen, meals and arguments
repeating like a scratched LP. Why did we abandon
our black clothes and move here?
To suck our teeth with big city superiority?
Or because the smog and concrete drained us, not even sex
helping for long? Why is it so hard
to hunker down someplace and make it home,
like the groundhogs happily tunneling
ankle-breaking holes out back?

Home

Alison Stone

Shingles, brick, wood, walls—
What makes a home?

Like a woman, a pipe
grows older.
Becomes less capable
of carrying others' shit.

A slow leak, months unnoticed.

We throw stuff in suitcases,
round up the animals

The insurance company's a god.
We are granted a motel. Then an apartment.

Told to make a list of loss,
I write:
Extra arguments
Home Depot instead of sex
Missing the climbing tree
break out its short-lived blooms.

I omit the crumbling walls in my dreams.

The names of birds in our borrowed elm?
Impermanence, of course.
            And *surrender*.

The house is a structure, painted blue.
It is not a metaphor.
It doesn't hold a marriage.

I will get a check,
new cabinets, a stove.

Yardless, the dog howls
behind our rented door.

Dogwood Window

Joannie Stangeland

After the assemblage Dogwood Meditations,
by Anita K. Boyle

Like butterfly wings pressed,
dogwood bracts fan as frail
and sheer as dancers' skirts
under glass and send me
back to that frayed summer
labeled *misunderstood*.

My sorry to the man
who followed you, helped me
across your past, a rope
bridge with every seventh
step missing, my dogwood
window the pink sapling

planted after you said
to take down the apple,
our understory myth
rewritten. Those crow years
and their starling nights now
outgrow ordinary,

fly at me paper-thin
with frayed edges, and why
has it taken this long
to touch the way I loved
you, like waiting for some
crumpled invitation,

handful of knobby seeds.
If I have lost too much
of myself, raked in fall
and hauled away, my leaves
light commas in the wind
like the wishbone drying

on the sill or the bones
that once belonged to wings
for home, if I have this
dogwood map, my true north
packed in boxes, the grief
still glitters in the grass.

I'm tired, dip pen & India ink on paper, by Clare Johnson

Finding the Girl from Guantánamo

Rebecca Francesca Reuter

The bus turned into an unmarked driveway, rocking me into the pillowy softness of Mamí's arm. I had no idea where we were until I saw the blue-gray island of concrete and metal appear—the Guantánamo bus station.

Our large, modern, tourist-class bus had left Santiago de Cuba before dawn and was traveling at a snail's pace. The two-hour journey to my mother's birthplace was a blur of fields with lemon-colored grass and the kelly-green tropical shrubbery of the Cuban countryside. When we passed a horse-drawn trolley with occupants sitting under a flapping blue tarp, perhaps on their way to work, school, or to visit relatives, I felt like we were in a time machine traveling back fifty years—but it didn't work as fast as those in the movies.

Not on our itinerary was the Guantánamo Bay U.S. Naval Base, over twenty miles past the town of Guantánamo. I say this because, when most Americans hear the word *Guantánamo*, they see images of prisoners clad in orange jumpsuits in front of slate gray walls mottled by the shadows of a chain-link fence. Most people may not realize that before it became a naval base, Guantánamo referred to the town where my mother was born and the bay it sits on. We were here to uncover the ghosts from my mother's past.

Mamí fled the island nation in 1961, when she was only sixteen years old. Fearing a life of oppression under Fidel Castro's regime, Abuela decided to place her daughters—Mamí and her older sister—alone on a plane from Havana to Miami. It was a decision made by many Cuban parents between 1960 and 1962, when an estimated 14,000 unaccompanied Cuban children were sent to the U.S. with the help of the Catholic Charities of Miami. This event would come to be called Operation Pedro Pan. A year after arriving in the U.S., Mamí would move with her sister and mother to Chicago, where her older brother had been living since before the revolution. Five years later, my mother would meet my father, an immigrant from Germany.

Planning for this trip started a few months after Obama was sworn in for his first term as President of the United States, in January of 2009. One of his first actions was to relax travel restrictions for Cuban Americans to visit relatives in Cuba. It was an announcement that left many in the Cuban-American community excited one way or another. I was living in Washington, D.C. at the time, working on a six-month project for the National Oceanic and Atmospheric Administration (NOAA). I was sweating through the swampy summer heat of July, looking forward to moving back home to cool, misty Seattle in less than sixty days, when Mamí called.

The conversation began as always with Mamí giving me a weather report for both wherever I was living and where she lived in Charlotte, North Carolina. I was half listening to her, half checking email and surfing the Internet, when she said, "I want to go to Cuba."

"That's nice . . . When are *you* going?" I asked after hearing nothing but heavy breathing on the line, signaling to my half-listening brain that she wanted a response.

"They say Obama is going to end the embargo. I want us to go soon, before it opens up," she explained.

"Now is not a good time for me," I said, thinking of the multitude of things I needed to do in the upcoming months: pack up my life in D.C., move back to Seattle, and deal with the ex-boyfriend I had broken up with before going to D.C., but let housesit so he could take care of my cats and figure out his next steps.

Mamí was serious. Her voice was deeper than usual and she spoke clearly, as if she were back in nurse mode updating a doctor about a patient. She feared that American tourists and developers would destroy the feel of old Cuba, or what was left of it, after fifty years of communism. She also wanted to exercise a special privilege few other Americans had. Since she was born in Cuba, and had a cousin to visit, she could be granted a general license by the U.S. Treasury Department. This was a weird consolation prize for being one of thousands of Cubans whose families had fled Cuba fearing political persecution after Fidel's revolution.

"But if I don't take you, you will never go," she said.

"You don't know that," I responded, defending myself from what I thought was a slight on my character. "Why can't you go alone?"

I had been telling Mamí to go on a solo trip anywhere since at least 2000, as a way to get her to stop complaining about how my father would never take her where she wanted to go. I thought I was making headway when she made plans for a solo trip to Spain for mid-September of 2001. But the 9/11 disaster on the East Coast extinguished those plans and they were never reignited.

"I want to share this experience with you," she added, revealing this was more than her wanting to dictate where I should be traveling. If only her voice weren't a cross between Desi Arnaz and Arnold Schwarzenegger. If only I wasn't so beaten down by years of her barking at me for this or that, with words that felt like military orders. Today, her tone sounded more like a plea, more Lucy than Ethel, and it melted a small corner of my heart.

"OK, I'll go," I said.

My eyes scoured the Guantánamo bus station to see if something looked familiar. I felt I should know Guantánamo after spending my childhood staring at black-and-white pictures from my mother's family. I was also looking for a place to get coffee and breakfast.

"Mamí, do you recognize anything?" I asked casually.

"No, not yet," she replied, her eyes also searching for the familiar after fifty years away.

I walked into the station. There was no smell of Café Cubano brewing, the syrupy sweet yet nutty espresso drink that would have tickled my cells back to life. No smell of freshly baked *pastelitos,* little pies of a savory ground beef wrapped in a flaky pastry dough and topped with a sweet glaze. I felt certain those items would have fueled me as I tried to figure out how to get to the town of Guantánamo. Mamí stood silently, gazing around with her big brown eyes, looking more like a lost puppy than someone searching for a way to get to her former home.

I stepped outside the bus terminal to find signs that would direct me to a taxi. When I didn't see any, I asked an official-looking guy wearing a khaki-colored uniform if he could help. He pointed to an empty driveway.

I became anxious. I was afraid we'd get stuck at the bus station or I'd have to make my mother walk to town, something neither she nor I would be thrilled about. I scanned the building for a telephone but didn't see one—but even if I did find one I wasn't sure who I would call. I had only the address of the bed and breakfast, not the phone number. I had no idea how far we were from town. The map of Guantánamo from our *Moon Cuba Handbook* didn't include the bus station.

"I should have figured getting a taxi would be hard. Guantánamo isn't a tourist destination," I said dejectedly into the air above my mother.

It was my passive-aggressive way of telling her I was pissed. She didn't seem interested in talking to "her people," she didn't have any suggestions, and she most certainly didn't want to take charge. Her urgency to travel to Cuba had not been reflected in her attitude or actions at any point since we'd arrived three days ago. I was beginning to wonder why she was on this trip.

In the instant it took me to scan the bus station a second time for help, a turquoise-blue Lada sedan pulled into the driveway. We quickly approached it as the driver was getting out of the car.

"Es un taxi?" I said eagerly.

"Sí, a tu servicio!" the man said with an authenticity that I knew wasn't just a rehearsed line.

A big grin of relief came over my face; I felt as if I'd just won the lottery. He was my hero, rescuing us from the station.

I jumped into the passenger's seat, Mamí got in back, and I gave him the address to the bed and breakfast.

I struck up a conversation with the taxi driver. I introduced us and shared the story that Mamí was visiting Guantánamo for the first time in fifty years.

"Ignacio Cuzco, a tu servicio," he said again.

"Cuzco?" Mamí blurted from the back seat. "Was your father a doctor?" She leaned towards the front.

My mother's sudden exuberance stunned me into silence.

She spoke rapidly. Her naturally serious face glowed with a happiness I had only witnessed when I was a child during Cuban family gatherings, as she told Ignacio the story about her stepfather, who had been a doctor in Guantánamo with a colleague named Cuzco.

"That was my uncle," he replied, "my father's older brother."

I was in awe. Here was my mother—the woman who has a hard time making friends and who *never* talks to strangers—talking to a stranger whose last name connected her with her past. It was a combination that injected a confidence in her that I hadn't witnessed since childhood, when she had been a confident mama bear protecting my brother and me, her cubs. A confidence that had mostly disappeared during my teenage years as the stresses of studying to be a registered nurse, working part-time, and taking care of the household took a toll on her. She kept the family together while Dad worked at his old-world trade of making violins on an old-world schedule of twelve-hour days, six days a week. It was during that time she had lost her pear-shaped hourglass figure to a barrel-shaped apple form through mindless eating. If only I had understood how that stress was the reason for her emotional outbursts and growing lack of confidence. If only I had seen what other people saw—a woman bettering herself while keeping a family together—perhaps I would have recognized more of myself in her and not rebelled so much as a teenager, and now, still, as a grown woman.

Within blocks from the station we were on a main road that led into town.

Mamí started to see familiar things. "Is this Cienfuegos Street?" she asked Ignacio.

"Sí," he replied.

"When I lived here it turned into mud when it rained," she chuckled, as we drove down the now concrete-paved arterial.

Ignacio slowed to turn left.

"Mira, Rebeca! Allí fue donde yo vivía después del casamiento de Mamí y Perucho!" she yelled, pointing to an apartment building where she had lived with her newly remarried mother.

Mamí seldom spoke Spanish to me. When I was a child the only Spanish she uttered were shouts of anger, or if she wanted to say something judgmental about someone while we were in public, like "Can you believe what that lady is wearing?" Now she was speaking Spanish to me as if she had done so all my life. I couldn't help but feel like a jilted child, sulking as I thought, *Now you talk to me in Spanish, when you had my entire childhood to teach me?* But I pushed away the petulant teenager within because I knew she was tapping into a part of her that had been asleep for fifty years. She was no longer a foreigner speaking a distant tongue in a faraway land. She was once again a *Guantánamera.*

The streets of Guantánamo were mostly deserted. A thin layer of dirt covered concrete sidewalks and roads, and the many potholes made them feel like unpaved country lanes. We passed deteriorating colonial-style buildings and empty storefronts. Nothing looked familiar to me as I tried to imagine the buildings newer and in black and white.

Recharged with Café Cubano and the snacks made by our hostess at the bed and breakfast, we walked towards the center of town. We were eager to look for vestiges of our family's roots. My mother's face scanned every building and street. She recognized the layout of the town, a simple grid, and confidently led the way. I trusted her instincts but, in case she got us lost, I'd torn the page with the map of central Guantánamo from the thick *Moon Handbook* and tucked it into my back pocket.

After a few blocks we found ourselves in the middle of town at Parque Martí. The park was bordered with benches and there was a wide concrete path. I envisioned families walking in groups during evening *paseos*, a tradition found in plazas throughout Spain and its colonies. I wondered if the tradition had survived the revolution. On this morning, the park was empty. We strolled around the plaza toward a small, single-steepled Catholic church painted yellow with white trim.

"This is Santa Catalina, where I was baptized," my mother said.

"Is that where Abuela and Abuelo were married too?" I asked, thinking of a picture etched in my memory of my grandmother and grandfather standing proudly in front of a medium-sized altar, their families flanking their sides. My grandmother was beautiful in a slender white satin gown, with a train draped around her feet, then cascading over a few steps below her. My grandfather, handsome in a simple black suit, looked poised, having married the most beautiful woman in Guantánamo. Which was mostly true, since only a few years before she had won the title of *Reina de Reinas del Oriente,* the queen of queens for the entire eastern province of Cuba. It was a picture I wished I could step into, to feel what it would have been like to live at the same time and place as my grandparents and so many of my relatives. Here I was, almost seventy years later.

"*Mira,* Rebecca, there is the movie theater," Mamí said, disrupting my daydream of being at my grandparents' wedding and throwing flower petals as they departed the church. She was pointing across the street at a 1950s-looking building, with light green arches in front of a dark green façade and a sign that said "Cine Huambo." Huambo is the name of a province and capital city in Angola, where Fidel Castro sent military support during its civil war from 1975 through the 1990s, so I thought it must have been a post-revolution building.

"Yup, that is a movie theater. How cool. Looks new," I responded.

"No, Rebecca, that is the theater I used to work at."

"Really?" I said.

My mother had told me many stories about this place. It was where she had her first job at age thirteen in 1956, around the same time Castro's men were organizing in the Sierra Maestra mountains about a hundred miles to the southwest. Her stories would describe sitting in a warm booth selling tickets or staying after work to watch movies. There was one story she told with delight, about the day she spent in the movie theater watching *Rock Around the Clock,* the first rock 'n' roll movie with Bill Haley and the Comets, over and over. I had a hard time imagining Mamí in a theater full of screaming girls, when the woman I grew up with was reluctant to go out and enjoy music or even go out with friends.

I knew this theater was family. In fact, my great-grandfather's half-brother had built it. However, it didn't look like the old-fashioned theater I had in my mind's eye. I was disappointed at its plain looks. My imagination had created a building with an old-style marquee that sat above a small set of doors and a ticket booth, like a miniature Chicago Theatre. Nevertheless, I felt a sense of pride knowing that a piece of my family history was still standing. It was a small victory against Castro's revolution. And from the look on my mom's face, she felt it too.

I felt in synch with Mamí as we played detective, looking for clues from our family's past. Our three-day visit to my mother's home town began to peel away at the layers of experience that had transformed the girl from Guantánamo into my mother. The layers created by living in a new country, learning a new language, adopting a new culture. The layer created when she married a man whose German language and culture were also different.

As we walked the streets, discovering places I'd only seen before in old family photographs, I watched the girl from Guantánamo re-emerge. I felt a connection to my mother I hadn't felt since childhood. I was coming home as well.

February, dip pen & India ink on paper, by Clare Johnson

Woodstoves and Outhouses

Angie Trudell Vasquez

Grandchildren fly on the rope swing
out back. She waits stirs the beans,
keeps the fire going.

What lies beneath her hands?

Wood smoke slips from a black belly stove,
red cinders fume from the night before.
Heat vibrates towards three boys in bed.
One raises his tousled head,
sees his Mom poke the embers
with a iron rod as tall as she is long.

What grows from her exhale?

Clean socks, shoes, pants—
three sets hang on wooden pegs.
Quesadillas warm metal lunch pails.
Square shoulders trod to school.
Boys with no father but a mother,
old oak in high winds
with roots deep and green.

What apple bouquet greets her nose?

Open the world
to bumblebee tongue
breath of pollen, breathe.

What flavor rose?

Her sons go come back, go come back.
Greets them with her mulberry trees,
vermillion roses, thinning hair,
flowered house dresses, aprons.

Called Out by Bulbuls

Diana Woodcock

There are hundreds of ways to kneel
and kiss the ground.—Rumi

Today I found yet another way
to kneel and pray—set out
a shallow pan filled with water,
a birdbath for the bulbuls.

Got quiet and still,
shut out the unbearable world
to be at home with white-eared softbills,
Pycnonotus leucotis, those precocious

socialites. Together we praised
the silent earth, her dark loam,
mold and sod, dust and dew.
I learned from the bulbuls to do

nothing but sit and sway
on a branch of bougainvillea all day,
just being. Doing nothing,
yet nothing left undone.*

Abstained from weeding, the heart bleeding
for the most common green shoot.
Quiet and still, just sitting and being,
considering how the politics of speed

deprives us of our natural habitats.
This little coastal town turned
upside down, thanks to oil and gas,
air and water pollution.

I sat and meditated, the solution
not so far-fetched—escape the blind
process of proliferation—
participation in third-world

exploitation and pollution.
In solitude and solidarity
with bulbuls, a clarity,
a sense of finitude overwhelms me.

The bulbuls call like chimes
to one another—a sound-map of this
desert town, songline from aridity to sea.
No mountains and moors,

nothing here but low desert terrain,
dunes shifting toward the sea
(a saline body on three sides of me),
and the miswak tree—fruit

upon which bulbuls love to gorge.
The urgency of Carson's silent spring
surrounds me—everything but the bulbuls
and palm doves gone silent.

Holding still, folding into leafy shade,
I—like the bulbuls—fill myself again
with the breath of leaves,
all that sustains me.

**Tao Te Ching*

Homecoming

Carolyne Wright

I'll come back dry-eyed from vacation,
back to business: Seattle and what suits it,
gray. Once I said I'd like to move out
on myself, return to find the premises
swept and empty. The usual parable—
the shabby spirits, panicked at the exit
of old thoughts, try to sneak back
with the new, vying with me to pay
seven times the rent.

I'll give in,
sublet the nightmare dwellings
to their familiar occupants,
jettison expectations, self-
addressed, enveloped thinking;
and race my shadow for the exit.

Grant me a few moments for the givens,
those gifts wrapped in chameleon skin.
You'll be there, alert and nervous
as a horse's ears, your voice
clinging to mine from the far end
of the line.

I'll say, Out there
the road took unexpected detours,
crossed bridges you can't get to
from the highway. My own reflection
was complete. I grew unexacting
in my touch as air, made love
a matter of kissing
and letting well enough alone.

You'll reply,
I dreamed safety into the arm's-length
of your letters, learned how dusk lingers
under hemlocks, tried to be loyal.
And me: Loyalty, that leaning of the heart,
indeed. Can we give each other
what we really need?

I'll give what I've brought—
miles of roadway, long walks
under broad-leafed shade, words
beating at my head with urgent wings,
a new kindness learned when a man's
failing love stirred me: private joys
that give us back ourselves, friends
showing each other the gentle way out.

The Last House on Pacific

David J.S. Pickering

My brother Kenny has a big scar
from the burn he got sleeping
behind the oil stove. Now he sleeps
in the kitchen, and the refrigerator hums
in his dreams every night.

I slept last night in Mom and Dad's fighting.

Today I'm up before anyone, a secret agent
slipping past the empty bottles, cats,
stacks of magazines, dad's work boots,
our dog that chews himself raw.

Anything can explode.

Mom and Alberta did their roots yesterday—
Lady Clairol auburn rust-bloody in the sink.
The kitchen smells like hair dye, broiled meat,
Aqua Net, cigarettes. A tube of Avon Red
Romance lies tipped on its side.

Kenny's steady sleep-breathing blends
with the stove clock's electric grind;
the quiet is sugar on my cereal.

Dried ketchup on the table
looks like a scab.

Adobe, Taos, with Painting in Window,
chalk, pastels, on paper by Rebecca Pyle

The Boneyard

Terry Sanville

Claudia Bannon pushes the screen door back and crosses the cookhouse porch. Her boots make muffled thuds with each step. A full moon has turned the oak-studded valley and side canyons a ghostly blue. She thinks about grabbing her Winchester, but decides to let the coyotes have their fun. She moves slowly, tired from a day of scraping down grease-encrusted grills and swabbing out.

As she ambles past the barn, her palomino whinnies. She calls to it in the midnight: "Easy there, Blondie. It's jus' me." Claudia follows the ranch road upslope, her breaths coming in white puffs. Ahead, the boneyard lies strewn across the hillside, black objects against silver grass: old cars, trucks, combines, tractors, graders, loaders, washing machines, tires, bedsprings. The ranch's history lies bare and broken before her.

Christ, I've lived here close ta forty years . . . and . . . and tonight could be ma last. She climbs onto a John Deere's form-fitting seat and stares at its engine, black holes where pistons had once pumped. As her breathing slows, the crickets find their song. *It's been a good run, a damn good life out here. Who knows, maybe the new boss will be okay . . . but a woman? What the hell were they thinkin'?*

She slides from the tractor seat and moves downslope to the rusted shell of a '59 Cadillac. Field mice burrow into the weeds as she approaches. In 1972, Claudia and Chester had made out in that Caddie, the night before he left. He'd brought along a couple longnecks and they'd thrown a saddle blanket across the still-usable back seat.

"Pop was going to restore this thing and give it to me for college," Chester told her.

"Ya gotta be kiddin' . . . this heap's more your mama's style."

"I know, but she didn't stay around long enough to . . . "

"A Cadillac's a stupid car for the Carrizo Plains. It'll be rusted to nothin' in a few years."

"What about you? Are you going to be worn to nothing? Out here cooking for ranch hands with nobody to . . . "

"Maybe I will . . . 'en . . . maybe I won't. It's none of your concern."

"What do you mean, not my concern? We've been going together for—"

Claudia shut him up with a kiss. He had the softest lips of any man she'd been with. But none of them loved the plains like her, and she always ended up by herself, in the tiny room off the cookhouse with her growing library of books on Indians, geology, North American birds, and a collection of arrowheads from the Caliente and Temblor Ranges.

Claudia picks her way across the moonlit hillside to the skeletal remains of a Beachcraft Baron, its twin engines lost to salvage. She studies the valley below, half expecting to see the plane's twinkling lights bounce along the airstrip, long since reclaimed by prairie grass. *The boss couldn't fly worth beans. I thought he'd take out the ranch house . . . 'specially on nights with the fog in.*

Frank Hurley took short flights to Fresno and Los Angeles on business, and every once in a while to Santa Barbara to bring Chester back, for a day, a weekend, never long enough.

"You look a bit frayed at the edges," Chet told her the last time they'd talked.

"And you look slicked up and ready for town. I heard y'all got engaged."

"Her name's Jessica . . . Jess. We're moving to San Diego next month, getting hitched in June."

"Well, good luck with that. You gonna bring 'er out ta the ranch?"

Chester grinned sheepishly. "Someday, maybe. I don't want the Carrizo to scare her off."

"I'll cook up one hell of a spread. Have ya told her about me?"

"Telling the woman I'm going to marry about an old girlfriend is not—"

"Who you callin' old?"

They'd both laughed but Claudia knew her looks had faded: gray streaks ran through her dark hair and gravity played havoc with everything else. The incessant winds and broiling summers had dried her face, adding crow's feet around her gray eyes and spider-web wrinkles to her russet cheeks.

A few weeks later, Frank had come in for a landing too low, clipped a sycamore and slid the Baron into the ditch. He walked away from the wreckage, but gave up flying. They hauled the Beachcraft to the boneyard and Chester stopped coming home.

Claudia climbs into the plane's cabin, works the corroded controls, and tries to ditch Chester from her mind. *I shoulda flew the coop. But this place had already grabbed hold . . . started likin' the sweet lonesome better than the company of field hands.*

On hot days during the wheat harvest, she'd driven the pickup loaded with the noonday meal into the northern hills. The field crew and combine operators gathered around the truck. Glad to get away from them, she drove south toward the Cuyama Valley, taking the long and slow way home.

The men steered clear of me by then anyway, except for that fool, Toby. Claudia jumps down from the plane's cabin and moves past a collection of rusted bedsprings. She'd been well into her 40s when they'd hired on Tobias Moran. She'd kidded Toby about being one of them Mormon pioneers from Utah. "Christ, ya got a family with seven wives hidin' around here somewheres?"

He grinned. "I haven't even found one . . . and keeping

that many women happy would be near impossible."

"Have ya ever tried . . . er . . . I mean . . . gettin' married?" Claudia felt her face burn. Toby was sure easy on the eyes.

"Oh yeah, got close a few times but nothin' took."

"Huh."

She helped him clean out the former ranch manager's stuff from the house, hauled it to the boneyard to rot in the sun. That summer, after lights out, they'd meet there, strip naked and lie in the darkness on an old mattress. They let the lupine-scented winds blow over them, stare at the stars and take their time. As the months passed, she realized she'd finally found someone who loved the Carrizo, who wasn't always talking about someplace else. But it didn't last.

On a wet winter afternoon while climbing the ridge, his horse slipped on the slick clay and rolled. They buried Toby on the hilltop, a serpentine rock cairn marking the grave. She can see it from her cookhouse and wonders if he was her last chance to get close.

Striding back to her room, Claudia showers then unbraids her long hair and brushes out the more salt-than-pepper mass. She slips into a flannel nightgown and crawls under wool blankets, the sheets deliciously cold. *Better get some shuteye . . . five hours 'til breakfast.* But her mind won't loosen its grip on consciousness. She clicks on the light and reads, a new wildflower book written by some University egghead. *I know more about where ta find these plants than any of them professors. But I'm jus' a cook . . . and what are they gonna do with a cook if this place quits being a ranch?*

Frank had suffered a heart attack and retired to So Cal in the mid-90s. His silent partners in Los Angeles slowly abandoned ranch operations: stopped growing wheat ten years back, and cut the cattle heard to a couple hundred head, next to nothing for a 30,000-acre spread. Then the owners trucked in tule elk from the San Joaquin. Claudia liked to ride Blondie into the northern hills and watch them run across the grassland, flowing like a magic carpet. She'd figured the owners would bring in hunters and run the ranch as a shooting camp. But that never happened and the herd grew.

The boneyard also grew as the barns and sheds emptied while the owners expanded the vacant ranch house, outfitted it with new furniture and appliances, added a swimming pool and Jacuzzi.

Well at least I'll find out tomorrow . . . don't know what I'll do if they fire me . . . could never move ta town . . . drive me crazy. She clicks off the light and dreams of being surrounded by city traffic, naked, laughed at for her age, for her prairie ways.

Awaking with a shudder, Claudia dresses quickly and slips into the cookhouse. Within an hour she has coffee, oatmeal, scrambled eggs and bacon, and fresh biscuits with honey and butter waiting for the crew. They stumble in, sleepy, complaining, nervous. She cooks for five: herself, Ernie the foreman, and three cowboys.

"So Claudia, we got another queen bee on the ranch today," Ernie jokes.

Buster grins. "Yeah, Clauds, you better hope the new manager likes lumpy oatmeal."

Their laughter rattles around the cookhouse. She stands over them, a pot of scalding coffee clutched in a mitted hand. The crew shuts up.

"So what's her name?" Claudia asks, "and when's she gettin' here?"

"You musta really been snoring," Erick says. "They pulled in last night, late, she and her husband and two girls. They call her Christie."

"Huh." *Sounds like some yuppie . . . kids probably named Ashley and Tiffany.*

"She said she'd join us for breakfast," Ernie says. "So I hope y'all wore your best undies."

"She say anything about our jobs?" Claudia asks.

"Nah. We'll find out soon enough."

Claudia pours cream into black coffee, listens to their idle chatter and munches a biscuit. *Maybe I could visit ma sister in Missoula. Haven't seen her in ten years . . . haven't been back to Montana in twice that long.* The cookhouse door opens and a slender blonde woman enters, wearing a sleeveless blouse, smiling. "Good morning, good morning."

The crew mutters their welcome.

"I'm Christine Wilkinson, but you can call me Christie." She sits at the table next to Ernie.

"What can I get ya for breakfast?" Claudia asks. *Jeez, I'll bet she'll want yogurt with granola.*

"I'll have some of your famous oatmeal . . . with brown sugar if you've got it."

Claudia stares at her to see if she's making fun of the oatmeal but only gets a bright smile in return. *She's got hair the color of ma pony's tail . . . and that skin's gonna burn, burn, burn. Can't be more than thirty-five.*

Claudia sets a bowl of thick meal in front of Christie along with a brown box of C&H and a carton of cream. But Christie gets up, grabs a cup from the rack and pours herself coffee. The men are quiet. *This babe's way too pretty for these cowpokes. And she's gonna be their boss?!*

"Thanks for letting me join you. Ted, that's my husband, is fixing our kids' breakfast, so this is a real treat for me."

Buster asks: "So you gonna be livin' in the manager's house, ya know, full time?"

Christie grins. "Yeah, you guys are stuck with us. Ted took a sabbatical from USC and I'm . . . well, I'm here until the owners say otherwise."

Ernie asks: "So just what do the owners have in mind for the ranch?"

"Why don' we let her eat before we pounce," Claudia says and gets a grateful look from Christie. The men go back to their muttered conversations.

Claudia slides onto the bench next to her. "We're all

jumpy about what's gonna happen. For some of us old timers, changin' things is damn tricky."

Christie nods, her mouth full of oatmeal.

I can feel it . . . she's gonna sack us all with a hardy handshake and fare-thee-well. Claudia slurps coffee and stares at her reflection in the cup.

"Your hair's really pretty," Christie says. "I wish I could braid mine like that . . . but it's too thin."

Claudia can't remember the last time a woman gave her a compliment. "I got hair like my mama. She showed me how to do all sorts of fancy braids . . . long before it became high fashion."

"Maybe you can show me sometime. My girls' hair gets so dirty and I'm gonna have to braid it or chop it off."

"Sure, jus' come over between meals and I'll show ya . . . that's if I'm still workin' here."

Christie frowns. "Yes, well I'd better get my little speech out of the way so that you folks can get on with it."

The men have gone quiet, unable to hide their eavesdropping. Christie stands and goes to the head of the table.

"First, let me compliment Claudia on a fine bowl of oatmeal . . . better than my own Nana's."

Claudia feels her face flush.

"Some of you may have noticed the name of the ranch painted on the side of my truck. It's not 'Oak Hills Ranch' anymore; it's 'Oak Hills Ecological Reserve.' The owners have signed a conservation easement with the State that sets out what can happen on this land and what can't."

"So you gonna keep runnin' cattle?" Buster asks.

"Yes, but we need to study how large the herd can be and still preserve the land's resources."

Claudia scans the men's faces, sees confusion rather than relief.

"I think what they're askin'," Claudia says, "is do they still got jobs?"

"Yes."

Claudia can almost feel a collective sigh from the men.

"But we may need to change how we do some things," Christie continues, "manage the herd differently so that we don't overgraze and cause erosion, maybe try some different breeds."

"Cattle out here gotta be tough as the land itself," Ernie says.

"Hell, I don' care what kinda cattle I work," Erick cracks, "jus' so's I get paid fer it."

"I'll be talking with all of you in the upcoming days about what's been done in the past and where we can make improvements."

"What about growin' wheat?" Claudia asks.

"For now, we're keeping the northern hills as habitat for the tule elk and pronghorn. But there are other locations where we might experiment with dry land farming."

Christie glances at her watch. "I've got to get back to my kids; it's their first day at a new school. But I plan on meeting with you at breakfast for a while to get to know this place, hear your stories. Before I go, Claudia, could you show me the kitchen?"

Claudia feels the numbness start at the back of her neck. *This is it. At least she didn't sack me in front of the others.* The two women move to the far end of the room and stop in front of the fire pit. Claudia folds her arms across her chest and blurts: "Look, I know it's stupid to pay a cook to feed just four ranch hands. All I ask is that ya give me a little time ta clear out and get settled somewheres else."

A confused look flashes across Christie's face. "You think I want to fire you?"

"Well . . . yeah. It makes sense, don' it?" She stares at the blonde woman. *Could I have read this wrong? Did I just screw myself?*

"No, it makes no sense," Christie says. "We can get cowhands anywhere to work the herd. But finding a good cook to prepare meals for the nature groups that'll be staying at the ranch . . . that would be hard."

"Huh." Claudia eyes Christie warily. "So . . . so how big are these groups y'all talkin' 'bout?"

"Maybe twenty, thirty at a time, all city slickers like me, wanting to taste home-on-the-range cooking."

"Jesus peaches. I haven't cooked for that many since the last harvest."

"Is that a problem? I can get you help if you need it."

"Naw, I kin handle it." Claudia feels the ends of her mouth tugging upward.

"And that big bedroom next to the kitchen in the main house," Christie continues. "It's yours if you want it. I've heard you've got quite a library and could use the space."

"Yeah, I collect books on birds and plants and stuff. More space'd be great."

"Well then, it's settled. I can help you move in this afternoon."

"Nah, don' need no help . . . but thanks. I gotta sort through ma junk."

Christie smiles and lowers her voice. "You know, you're the only other woman anywhere near this place. I'm not used to living in the boonies. Us girls got to stick together, don't you think?"

"Yeah . . . yeah, sure. You got it, boss."

Claudia returns to her tiny room and stares at the scarred and tattered furniture. *I should haul this junk to the boneyard . . . and maybe, jus' maybe, I kin finally tell somebody 'bout Chester and Toby.*

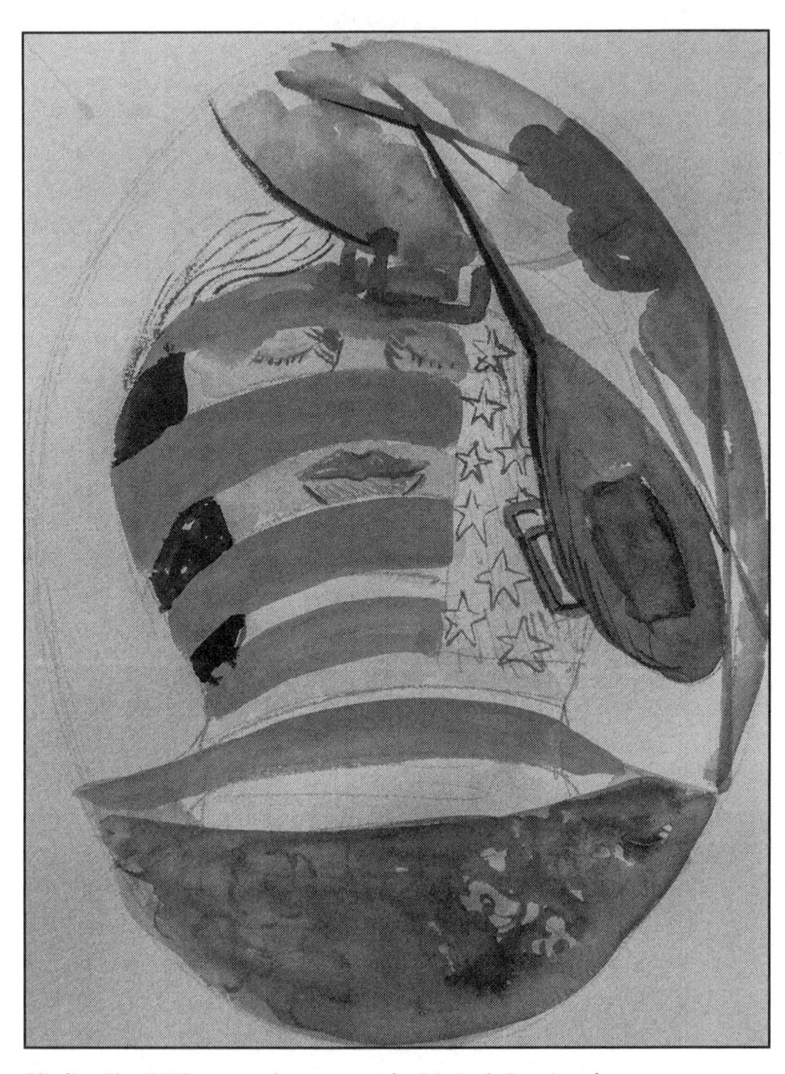

Blinding Flag, 2017, watercolor on paper by Maria de Los Angeles

Maria de Los Angeles:

Breaking Through Barriers

Susan Noyes Platt

When Maria de Los Angeles was an art student in the MFA program at Yale University, her obvious Mexican heritage led her teachers to suggest Frida Kahlo as her predecessor! Actually, if you look at her work, what you see is German Expressionism as an inspiration, with artists such as George Grosz and Kathe Kollwitz as mentors. Look a little closer and you can recognize a love of classical old masters such as Giotto, whose work she saw in Italy last summer. Her stunning drawings and watercolors urgently address our current immigration crisis, particularly the shattering emotional trauma of U.S. Immigration and Customs Enforcement (ICE) raids on families.

Maria de Los Angeles draws with ink or watercolor on two types of paper: printmaking (which is manila-colored) and drawing paper (which is white). Sometimes she draws figures on the lighter-colored drawing paper, cuts them out, and then glues them onto the manila-colored paper on which she also draws. The resulting two tones create a dynamic that reinforces the primary theme of her work—the constant terror of a family being torn apart as ICE officials raid homes, courts, workplaces, public spaces, and even cars—looking for undocumented immigrants to detain and deport.

But she doesn't use a simplistic formula to create her work. The white people are not always cut out with white paper, nor are all the Latino figures manila-colored. That is of course because that is how real life is. In fact, some ICE officials are Latinos, and some Latinos are light-skinned (as is Maria herself). Her use of the two colors of paper creates a tension, emphasizing the sense of fear and hostility immigrants confront daily amidst escalating deportations.

She adds text as well in her work—tiny words like "My America" or "Our America" emerge in bubbles from the mouths of ICE agents; or she writes longer texts around the edge of the drawing, such as racist taunts and clichés. She breaks through restrictions and conventions in her art, just as she would like to see barriers between races break down.

De Los Angeles frequently depicts ICE agents swooping down from the sky to threaten families trying to protect themselves. Intense networks of lines evoke their anguish as they cower in terror. But sometimes salvation itself swoops down from the sky to rescue someone from the agents on the ground.

She also creates garments. She sews paper together, and paints them with confrontational slogans, such as "illegal" and "undocumented." Then she takes a group of friends to do interventions, at places like the Trump Hotel, or she creates an "illegal fashion" show.

The most recent attacks on undocumented immigrants, led by the Trump administration, threaten to withhold federal funds from Sanctuary Cities. Leaders of Sanctuary Cities want to reduce the fear of deportation and possible family break-up among people who are in the country illegally, so that such people will be more willing to report crimes, use health and social services, and enroll their children in school.

Maria de Los Angeles's emotion-filled drawings and watercolors invoke the terrifying experience of ICE raids and move us to resist these oppressive, racist policies.

Home without Assimilation

Maria de Los Angeles

Many United States citizens have visited my home country, Mexico. They know it better than I do. I get gifts from Mexico mostly from my white friends who go there on vacation or who own homes there. They always tell me I can visit someday. I say yes, one day, "when I get my papers." The truth is that Mexico sits on the other side of the border, a border that separates me from my past. I am an example of the American Dream and the United States is my new home. I have achieved what my parents wanted. I am a resident of the USA; legal or not.

To many of us brought here by our parents, the American Dream is an inheritance—a possibility of the abundance that our parents could not provide us in our respective countries. Our parents migrated in hope of giving us a better future. Most immigrants believe that if they migrate and work hard, they can have a happy, simple life where the basic necessities are taken care of. Children are safe, have a home, and benefit from a good education.

We are known as the "Dreamers," or the "undocumented." An attempt by Congress to legalize us in 2001-2010 is known as the DREAM Act (Development, Relief, and Education for Alien Minors). It didn't pass, so in 2012 President Obama issued the Executive Order known as Deferred Action for Childhood Arrivals, or DACA, which gives us a renewable, temporary, two-year work authorization card, and, if we have an invitation, an opportunity to travel abroad.

In the 2000s, the idea of us having an education was considered a waste of time because we could not legally have jobs. But we continued to go to school in hopes that someday

Artist Portrait in Paper Dress, 2016, photo by Adrian Mendoza

there would be immigration reform. Our education was still something that we could strive to achieve. As undocumented children, we could not qualify for government financial aid; we could only qualify for private money and scholarships.

I was accepted to many University of California colleges; however I could not attend them due to lack of financial aid. Luckily I also applied to many private schools outside of California, one of them being Pratt Institute in New York. They gave me a partial scholarship for one year and I raised the rest of the tuition through sale of my artwork. I was then blessed with a full scholarship for the next two years.

I am proof that the American Dream is possible. As an un-legalized American, I completed an Associate in Fine Arts at Santa Rosa Junior College (California), a BFA in Fine Arts Painting at Pratt Institute (New York), and an MFA in Painting and Printmaking at Yale University School of Art (Connecticut).

I was smuggled into the USA at age eleven with my siblings while drugged on Tylenol PM because our "coyote" (smuggler) did not want us to speak to the border patrol in Spanish. In 2000, we moved to Santa Rosa, California, where I started seventh grade at Lawrence Cook Middle School, although a few months before I was enrolled in the second grade in Mexico. Transitioning to a new culture and new educational system was difficult. I had to work harder than my classmates, do extra credit, and make sure that I attended tutoring sessions. The idea that you are behind in school can sometimes be enough to propel you forward. If you know there is a deficiency, then you can address it. That is what I did.

I consider this country my home, although the legal system does not allow me to call it my home. Which brings me to ask, "Who gets to call this country theirs, and why?" I do not consider myself an immigrant anymore. I consider Mexico a place that will forever have strong roots in my heart, but

I do not know it as well as I know here. And legally I have been restricted from visiting Mexico since the day I crossed the border as an eleven-year-old.

I have felt marginalized since I was young. The first time I felt this feeling of not belonging was in middle school, when the kids who were born in the USA would make fun of us wetbacks. In high school, the most traumatizing experience was when a classmate, who did not know my legal status, would joke with other boys about "raping an illegal because no one would call the police." Or when I had jobs white men would say, "I want to speak to the one that speaks English." Those comments didn't really make me angry, but they hurt because those people had no idea who I was and am. I have a multiplicity of identities: I am here as an un-legalized citizen, but I also have the full cultural understanding and upbringing that any other kid in this country has.

Rumors of checkpoints and raids were part of our childhood. A common practice across the USA, they are announced on the radio, TV, Internet, and now on Facebook—a type of weather report. I never made drawings of my experiences and emotions as an immigrant until I attended Yale University. There I began creating images of those feelings. Feelings of not being home, of not being legalized. I became an artist.

I personally have only experienced the fear of a being swept up in a deportation raid; I have never actually been in one nor had any immediate family deported. But many of my friends have. Since the Obama and Trump presidencies, many families live in fear of being pulled apart by ICE.

Law enforcement has always scared me; I feel it at all levels, even when just interacting with a security guard. I feel like I don't belong, like at any moment I am going to be arrested. While traveling to New York City to study, and on my first flight across the country, I felt an intense panic. I never admitted this to anyone, but authority figures make me sick to my stomach. Perhaps that is why, when making drawings of border patrols, cops, and scenes of deportation,

I often feel sick. I take breaks between working sessions in my studio. I also know that making these drawings helps me deal with the trauma of being illegal. Many of my drawings of mothers being deported are not of my mother, but inspired by nightmares growing up and by stories I read online. It was not until recently that I stopped having nightmares about my family being pulled apart, but lately the nightmares have returned, especially now that nationalism and anti-immigrant sentiment is high. They are reaffirmed by the five million deportations since Obama, and those that add up like popcorn every day. I think of the border and its implications now, a border I dreamed my way across at age eleven, sound asleep and unknowing.

My whole knowledge of art was constructed here, though I feel excluded from western art history. While I was at Yale, during critiques, people would say, "She does not know German Expressionism because she is Mexican," or "She should know about Mexican art because she is Mexican," or "The use of color in her paintings is Mexican," or "She is a Mexican artist." Am I really? Am I culturally at home in Mexico or here, where I have been educated but prevented from fully knowing the history of the country I called home once and am legally barred from seeing again? I feel separated from knowing my own identity as an artist; I am suspended between the legal system and nationalistic neoliberal ideology.

While I crossed the border once, I am still on that line with its broken promises, suspended in an in-between space both legally and mentally. Culturally, I am more United States of America than United States of Mexico. Regionally, I am North American by birth. English has become the language in which I communicate best, but Spanish words are the ones that I like to roll around in my mouth; I love their taste. But I am an illegal immigrant, now and always, to the immigration enforcement system.

For me, assimilation means being proud of all sides of my identity, and having my humanity respected. Step one toward that respect is legalization of illegal immigrants and the end of this system of exploitation. To be multicultural is the true meaning of assimilation—to keep the accent, to dance the music, to cook the food. There is no one dominant culture to assimilate to.

I love this country! I am a person who has strong hopes that we can move forward, and change, and stop excluding others based on race and class lines. After almost seventeen years in America, I am still a faithful believer in the dream my parents had that I can build a home here, that my family can call this place home. But year after year my strength is tested. I am not ungrateful or angry with my parents for bringing me here by whatever means necessary; I am so happy they did. I was able to get a great education and become an artist. To become an artist is the biggest gift, one that has changed who I am as much as my legal status and experience of migrating here have. But while I plan to continue, as an artist, making images about my experience, I do not plan to continue being un-legalized. If I cannot call this country home, I will leave. I know the solution for one, myself, is not the solution for many, and that if I left, I would never see my family again. Once I leave, I can't come back.

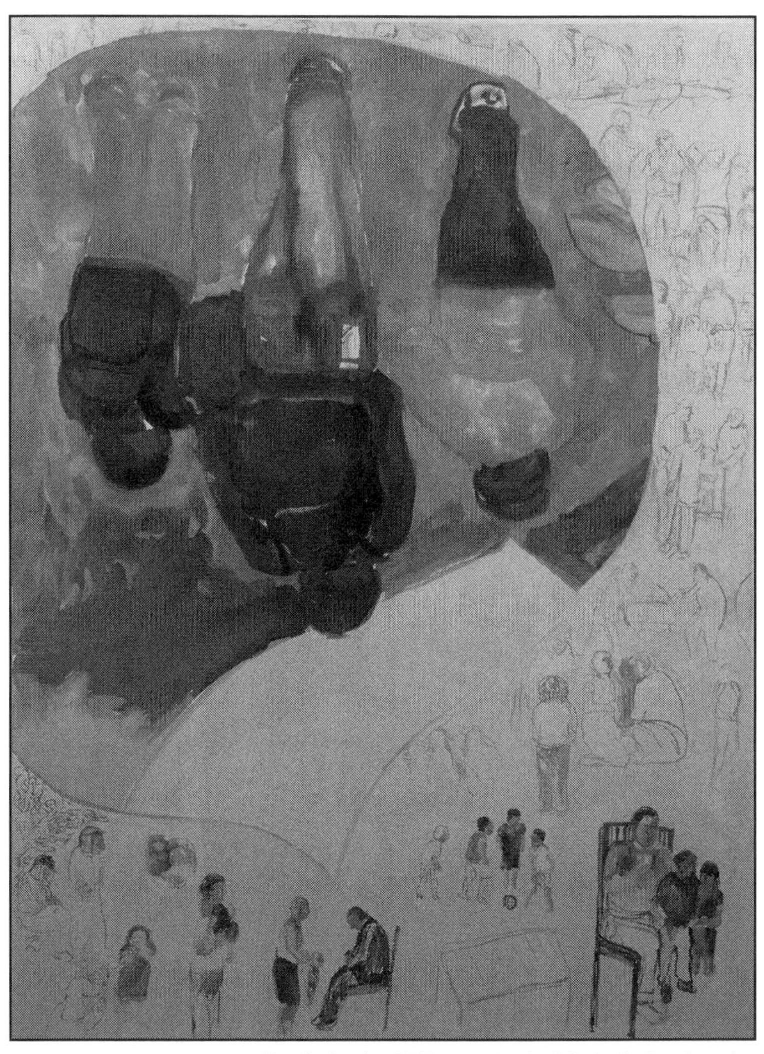

Family Stories, 2015, painting by Maria de Los Angeles

Still Life with Rain

Virginia Barrett

My rain today
—mine, I call it, because
it comes so little here

and don't precious things
make us ache to possess
them more? How to *write*

the sound of tires on a wet
road: a kind of textured
swooshing promises

its own risk. I hear a
crow; his feathers, a glistening
sable I imagine, hold

a haunting undercurrent
but hints of purple luster
invite melancholy, too. I washed

the windows this week, now
the storm washes them again. I
might have waited to see if

the weather report came
true, but I like my view to be
clear, looking out on this dead

end street which once merged
with another named after
a Mexican alcalde of Yerba

Buena murdered by a vigilante
—and yes, a murder is also
a family of crows. I live

alone, with ample time today
to admire Van Gogh's *Wheatfield*
with Crows, in a book borrowed

from the library: a menacing
blue sky, yellow-orange
field, black crows converging

like a great swarm of giant
locusts, and a red path, leading
nowhere . . . intensified

by thick green bands of
grass. One of his last paintings,
the text says, "it signals

his suicide," but to me it's
a manic comfort, the irrefutable
grandeur of the land.

Van Gogh said, "the painter of the future
is a colourist such as there hasn't
been before," in truth describing

himself—as I try between
looking to capture the day; what
do I want from the rain?

The Guest Bedroom

Sharon Hashimoto

The tabby flicks his tail
against the white nightgown,
head-bumping her legs, meowing
his distress at the stranger
sleeping behind the closed door
upstairs. She shushes the cat,
filling a glass at the faucet,
watching the water roil.
Standing bare-footed, she sips
and listens hard for a creak
or soft snore, imagines clean sheets
yielding to the weight of a body
on a bed, the pattern of hair
on a pillow. Because the cat
wants her lap, she sits in the kitchen—
the chair's four legs stepping
on moonlight. Her hands slowly
stroke the rumbling fur, the warmth
of its belly and breath.

"Typical nonsense as I try to write," drawing by Saint James Harris Wood

IX

Rants, Raves & Reviews

Alaskero
Memories
GULF OF ALASKA
Scale of Miles
OCEAN
ROBERT FRANCIS FLOR

Alaskero Memories

by Robert Francis Flor

Carayan Press, http://alaskero.carayanpress.com
ISBN: 978-0-9964694-8-7
2016, paper, 40 pp., $12.00

Reviewed by Maria Batayola

There is a delicious contradiction in the literary world that writers straddle, intentional or not, the universal human experience and the specifics that make it unique.

Robert Francis Flor straddles this world exceptionally well with his chapbook *Alaskero Memories*. Flor trumps the sins of reader presentism (viewing things through one's contemporary lens) by encasing his poetry with Filipino American immigration and labor history, and including historic and personal photos that enliven the poems.

A coming of age book, Flor recalls the elder Filipinos—colorful, rough and tumble—who influenced him when he worked for college money for four summers in Alaska canneries. He often lulls us with his poetic narrative, surprising us with a twist or a bit of wisdom in the last line.

Poet Oscar Penaranda spoke of "... the jazz-like rendering of *Alaskero's* "life in the trenches" replete with unforgettable and raw details of Alaska Cannery life . . . ." while Filipino American historian Dr. Dorothy Cordova observed "... Bob's poetry . . . a beautiful tribute to the Filipino Manongs who treated him like a surrogate son . . . ." I agree.

My only quibble, not quarrel, with Flor, is the layout of the poetry. In many instances, the poems are presented in paragraphs, denying the reader the visual cue, the space, to breathe in between the lines and take the time to absorb the full impact of the lovely imagery and pithy meaning of the short pieces.

A THOUSAND HORSES
OUT TO SEA
Erika T. Wurth

A Thousand Horses Out To Sea

by Erika T. Wurth
Mongrel Empire Press
133 24th Ave NW, Suite 103, Norman, OK 73069
www.mongrelempire.org
ISBN: 978-0-9972517-3-9
2016, paperback, 69 pp., $15.00

Reviewed by Thomas Hubbard

In *A Thousand Horses Out To Sea,* Erika Wurth has written a beautiful, painful story made of poems, a story lived over and over for years and years, in millions of variations by mixed blood NDNs and their friends in this America. It's a collection of vivid scenes in which most of us have sometime played a part. If your heart pumps any indigenous blood, or perhaps even if it doesn't, reading any one of these poems will bring a been-there grimace to your face or a nod of your head in affirmation.

Wurth's story starts early in her life—It started early in mine, too, and I remember chasing fireflies in the Indiana summer evenings with my white cousins. So this poem almost makes it rain.

Leaving the Glow

There are fireflies here,
and at sunset, they come out.
I think of my white cousins in New York,
how we chased them with jars
capturing them so we could watch them float,
and glow under our hands.

We were greedy and beautiful and even ideal,
our white hands and Indian hands praying the same way,

to the same light, our family watching from the dusty /
gray porch,
before everyone went off into their separate adulthoods,
leaving the glow of the evening far behind.

Unless you're a more perceptive reader than I, your first reading of this fine collection will register as just that: a collection of wonderful short poems, as visual as movies. If you only read it once, you got your money's worth. But read through it again, and pay close attention to the characters: I, you, she, he, etc.

You'll find them repeating, and come to know them a little. You'll see them interacting, and you'll know them a little better. You'll discover how all the poems are connected, and the characters as well. You'll see relationships come into focus.

These poems, this story, tells of love, but it also shows the physical, mental and spiritual violence that comes *with* love, coming to well-meaning people again and again, slipping in through fissures in their understanding, cracks in the structure of their family, chasms opened among their ancestors by the invaders . . . and opened sometimes by invaders being *among* their ancestors. The violence, just out of sight in most of these poems, emerges in a few, and in "Wild Blue Glory," emerges as a *need.*

I need someone to break me, shake me,
pull me apart. I need violence, blood and sap
running down my long, yellow arms . . .

Despite the fissures, the cracks, the chasms, one still must find a life and a love. Skin color or hair color seems so often to interrupt the search, however. Note (above) the "long yellow arms" of a mixed blood who lives out of the sun. The *mixed-blood* current running like a sensual river through these poems lends a shade of approach-avoid to the idea of crossing that race line. It becomes inescapable in the poem,

"In That Place That No Longer Exists."

I touched you in that place that no longer exists,
in those lost white apartment buildings behind /
  your father's house,
your sad, almost Indian face moving drunkenly /
  towards mine.

I gave you so little, and how you curved into yourself /
  when I left,
the memory of your cold white hands in my black hair /
  almost unbearable,
like something old and dusty . . .

Always, with the drinking, there is the danger, as in "Spinning Them," where Wurth identifies herself.

When the children are released into the waiting arms /
  of the strangers
who have already drank too much
I am, wherever I am, the strange dark woman in /
  the center,
holding them up and spinning them.

And when a love or a life ends, these characters must find another, and another, until time comes to set out to that sea not shown on maps. Wurth touches often on the important factor of Indian-ness, the factor always running beneath the surface and sometimes surfacing, as she explains in a gentle voice in "Fort Peck Girl."

On that night in the bar, she spoke about anger
and I touched my scars as the bodies wound all around /
  us, she and I
only just beginning to measure the distances that exist /
  between people
in bars, between everyone.

She, most beautiful Indian girl I've ever known. Fort / Peck girl, body
straight as an arrow in the soil, her mother's initials / tattooed on her
back, right beneath the great red wings of the / thunderbird stretching
poetically above.

Those wings floated down as I helped her into her / dress, yes,
the one she will wear at her altar, at his, at ours, the / one we wear
under all of our wings when we love enough to risk / bringing
down the first altar, the one that says we must worship

alone.

In such volatile lives, betrayal seems inescapable, and it shines through the story's fabric in "Smoke Billowing." Wurth describes herself figuratively, "Walking alone in the Chicago night, / my worn red heels echoing in these wild dusty streets . . ." And in the last stanza,

Yes, I am the woman we laughed about,
the tall, the yellow, angry dark haired woman,
I am full of your betrayal,
my face plastered on every window, every ancient black / door,
I'm selling mangoes, horchata, sex, phone cards;
just another lonely Indian, posing as everything else,
searching for fire, smoke billowing out of me like a / factory.

Then in "Safety Dream," the source of betrayal comes to light.

And you, and you, with your sleepy child bride on /
the couch,
her small blond head resting on your arm
you think of my darkness,
the way my Indian hair filled the hollow of your neck,
my moans, my cries . . . my cries . . . inside me
grandmother closes her eyes as you enter, saying
the only way this works for me is to forget.
Yes, forget, forget, forget your strange whisper that you /
loved me,
quiet now, go to sleep, join her world on the couch. That /
safety dream,
the one, the only one, I never knew.

These poems speak of love—love as it happens between and among people whose world has been fractured by centuries of invasion, whose ancestors have been dispossessed, murdered, shoved aside. The love in these poems is a love ruptured and stretched, ruined but still binding lovers, families, peoples together, pulling and pushing them with a force that can splinter their souls, a love shining painful neon from gritty saloons across the land, reaching from one generation to the next with tortured echoes that resound through the history of a people dreadfully wronged and nevertheless surviving while their blood mixes with that of their invaders in progeny caught between two colliding worlds.

Some readers may encounter a bit of frustration in lacing these characters and this story together. Most will see it as invigorating exercise. Youvery well may look back on reading this book, to realize it began your understanding.

Words From the Café

an anthology

Edited by Anna Bálint

Words from The Café, An Anthology

Edited by Anna Bálint

Raven Chronicles Press, www.ravenchronicles.org
ISBN: 978-0-9979468-0-2
2016, paper, 202 pp., $14.99
CD in book when ordered from Raven's website,
www.ravenchronicles.org/shop/

Reviewed by Martha Kreiner

Last fall was very, very hard. Not I-cried-on-the-weekends-but-held-it-together hard. More like, my-skin-hurts-and-even-cheddar-and-sour-cream-potato-chips-don't-taste-like-anything hard. Like my-arms-hang-like-clubs-from-my-body-and-the-light's-gone-out-of-the daytime hard. Like where my warm and open heart usually beats in my chest, shaking me just a bit from the inside, I no longer feel even hollowness. There is just a blank feeling—which isn't even a feeling—there is just a stale and barely breathable air, smelling the way I imagine the knotty, wired, dark middle of an android must smell, all sealed up and dustless, before someone plugs it in.

I did not, during those difficult months, wander into The Recovery Café, a clean and sober gathering spot in downtown Seattle, where Anna Bálint facilitates Safe Place Writing Circle most Friday afternoons, and where she also teaches classes. But I now feel I could have, and that it is a shame I did not. In the anthology *Words From the Café*, she has collected writing (and on the accompanying CD, actual voices) I urgently need to hear.

She features ten writers, introducing each with a verbal and photo portrait, and sprinkles other voices throughout. Running through them is what I first took to be humility. In "Cry and Transform," Taumstar writes, "Accomplishments?

/ Not everyone gets to accomplish much; " Allen Taylor writes "Even Halloween is a hard time;" and Megan McInnis says, ". . . [I]t's one thing to try to convince someone you're pathetic and crazy; now I have to prove I'm competent . . ." Mary Jo El-Wattar says, "I am good at saying good morning to neighbors;" and Steve Torres writes, ". . . I'm thankful that I did not hurt or kill someone else." Not a boastful bunch.

The more I read, however, the more I realized humility isn't what I was encountering; it was trust, the trust of the writing circle these authors create and share in, and the courage it gives rise to, to be just exactly who they are on any given day. Sometimes, that person is joyful and curious, as when Shelby Smith writes, "Remember somersaults. / Remember that roundy feeling . . . / Find out about bees." Sometimes that person is a keen observer of language, as when Bang Nguyen describes exactly how lost his name is, in translation: "In my language it's not even said this way. There's a whole lot of accent marks missing in your American language. The *A* should have an accent mark like a bamboo hat over it. It's from the French Indo-China times and makes the *A* sound low, then high, then low again, all in one letter."

And sometimes that person says it just like it is, plainly and without softening it, and it is difficult to read, as when Dana Nelson Dudley opens with, "I would love to jump off / the little, low Fremont Bridge, / with its paint fairly fresh still." Such a specific and terrible wish. But he hasn't jumped off the bridge; instead, he has written about it, given voice to wanting to, in trusted company, and then shared it with us.

If you have ever made a grave mistake, and followed it up with even more terrible behavior; if you have ever been lonely; if you have ever been so lonely, the mute expressions of passers-by hurt you; if you have ever vacuumed your bedroom, or washed your hair, or made an egg salad sandwich, or swung your legs to the side of the bed and sat up, then knew with your whole body you had reached the exact limit of what you could accomplish that day; there is solace for you here, and truly fine human company. I thank Anna

Bálint and the courageous authors at The Recovery Café for walking so publicly; now the rest of us don't have to be alone.

Selector and Hobbyist
RUXANDRA CESEREANU
Foreword by
MARGENTO
MOODS
& WOMEN & MEN
& ONCE AGAIN
MOODS
AN ANTHOLOGY OF CONTEMPORARY
ROMANIAN EROTIC POETRY

Moods & Women & Men & Once Again Moods, An Anthology of Contemporary Romanian Erotic Poetry

Edited by Ruxandra Cesereanu, with a Forward by Margento
Tracus Arte (Romania), 2015, http://www.tracusarte.ro/
Calypso Editions, www.calypsoeditions.org
2017, paper, 210 pp., $18.99

Reviewed by Elizabeth Myhr

When I read a book this outstanding, it makes me wonder why I bother to read poetry written in English at all. I don't mean to belittle the English language when I say this. I simply mean that poetry in translation often carries such an electric charge, such a wonderful energy, that it's worthwhile to stop reading English-language poets for a while and dive into what the rest of the world has on tap.

The poets in this amazing erotic anthology take the kinds of emotional and psychological risks that Americans (losing ground in the haze of backward politics, to put it lightly) can only dream about—perhaps in a future that includes a renewed blossoming of intense human fervor. We shall see. For now, if you are a writer, or an avid reader, buy this book immediately and devour it. It is a source of intellectual hope, and is stupendously, miraculously good. Its poets are bold, curious, and so very much alive! They are here tumbling through literature with all their might.

Here's Teodor Dună, 35, considered a visionary of his generation:

As The Salt Murmus In The Sea

as the salt murmurs in the sea, so does your heart

you take me in your arms, tell me we are equally cold,
meaning the cold is for both of us.
we almost touch, you show me your wounds, /
so well-nursed,
you've taken such good care of them,
you've tamed and groomed them,
they resemble pets—and we gaze at each other /
through overturned
bottles.

you rest your wounds next to me
and rested we carry entire banquets.

this night is too ancient, you say.
and your hands seem to offer handfuls
of frozen birds—you ask me
to dress you in wild vine,
I cannot I tell you,
I show you how rooted we are the long rest that remains.

I very nearly take you in my arms,
I very nearly recoil from your wounds.
and we gaze at each other, how else but through /
overturned bottles.
not a word from our lips.
and as the salt murmurs in the seas, so does your heart.

And here is Magda Cârneci, 61, who wishes her work "to cast light onto the bloody inside of today":

from *Love Stories, (fragments)*

The yellow angel enters the blue angel.
An azure flash! Oh, the froth of light, the starry lace!
He fills her crystal glass with hot, superhot dynamite
and seals himself deeply inside. A red, burning filament

slowly making room, downwards, pushing to the core,
Making room, room, room, then depositing
himself in the sanctuary. A drop.
She awaits him behind a small golden door lined /
with moist purple.
Reddish, bluish dewy purple!
Oh velvet fire, sweet abyss, undulating sea of plush fur,
veil devouring silk, smothering avalanche of /
cotton candy,
corrugated fold to the other world, fleshy sky of the deep.
He knocks and knocks softly, softly, then harder /
and harder.
Meanwhile, he forgets his way. He knocks, keeps /
on knocking.
Nobody replies, nothing. He knocks, pounds. And /
forgets everything.
Falls Collapses. Is lost.
Blind, surrounded by terrifying magnetic darkness.
Feels just the scorching heat. Fire.
Meltdown. Disaster. He gives up the ghost.
There on the threshold.
It's only then that the blue angel opens up
her delicious and beautiful palate and explodes . . . .

Need I say more? Buy this book before it's gone.

HOLA AND GOODBYE
UNA FAMILIA IN STORIES
DONNA MISCOLTA
UNCORRECTED PROOFS. NOT FOR RESALE OR DISTRIBUTION.
PLEASE DO NOT QUOTE WITHOUT COMPARISON TO THE FINISHED BOOK

Hola and Goodbye: Una Familia in Stories

by Donna Miscolta
Carolina Wren Press
120 Morris Street, Durham, North Carolina 27701
https://donnamiscolta.com
ISBN-978-0-932112-64-4
2017, paper, 285 pp., $17.95

Reviewed by Angie Trudell Vasquez

I have been a voracious reader all my life but I have never encountered a book like Donna Miscolta's *Hola and Goodbye: Una Familia in Stories.* I have never seen my own family's experience laid out in such great detail, understanding, and humanity.

Hola and Goodbye is Miscolta's second novel (the first was *When the de La Cruz Family Danced,* Signal 8 Press, 2011), and it received the 2015 Doris Bakwin Award for Writing by a Woman. It is a riveting collection of interlinked stories told mostly from a woman's point of view in the first or second person. The women are center stage throughout the book and central to the heart of most of them is Lupita, the matriarch, the first woman in her family to come to the U.S. Lupita's story opens the collection. Not being able to speak English when someone immigrates is common. What is uncommon is how Miscolta describes Lupita's thoughts about Spanish versus English:

> . . . It was music she had yet to find in her new home, a town almost as dusty as her old one, but with no poetry to save it. There was only English.

Lupita's experiences, and those of her offspring and their offspring, make for a compelling read. But their tales of assimilation are sometimes painful to read because I recognize my own parents' experiences and those of my aunts and uncles; and because I recognize myself and the experience of being The Other. Characters in the book start by not speaking English fluently, but some of them completely lose the ability to speak Spanish by the third generation. Millie, one of Lupita's daughters, struggles to make her children mind her, and Miscolta reveals Millie's inner dialogue in a haunting passage:

> . . . She used her Spanish when she was angry at them or when she talked about them to her sisters or her mother. She used it at them or over them, never to them, so they never learned to speak it. She hated that about them.

Miscolta writes a scene describing a situation many women go through together, but rarely discuss:

> Lupita dragged Rosa to the bathroom and positioned her doubled-over body on the toilet. Rosa continued to moan softly while Lupita, midwife to her miscarriage, massaged her neck and shoulders, moved her hands along the length of her spine to press on her lower back.

Women have been taking care of each other for centuries. This knowledge is carried down sister to sister.

> The door opened and Lupita came back in, knelt down next to the tub, and took a sponge to Rosa's shoulder.

These types of occurrences are usually whispered about when the kids are out of the room, and then only to a select few. This scene is written with deep empathy and an understanding of the nuances of the situation. Sometimes what is not said is just as important as what is being said, and Miscolta makes these characters come alive on the page.

To find a book where women are the main focus throughout, Latinas in particular, is a rare find. To find a story of immigration so original and believable is even rarer. All these stories ring true to me—the characters resemble real people I grew up with and observed closely and at a distance. I see myself in Lupita's offspring. I recognize my sisters and cousins.

To hear about the Camacho family's struggles, to read another immigrant family's story is good for those of us who looked for our reflection on television or in popular culture in vain. Food makes an appearance in these pages from the beginning to the end. A ghost makes an appearance.

A reader roots for the characters, holds their breath, and at times laughs out loud, at least I did. Like Amy Tan, Miscolta delivers a portrait of people rarely covered in literature and appears to do so effortlessly, while providing real insights into what motivates people. She offers sage advice too, ". . . life was not about running away but running toward something . . ."

As both a second and third generation Mexican American, I want to go out and buy this book for all the women in my family: there is great healing here.

Rules for Walking Out
Crysta Casey

Rules for Walking Out

by Crysta Casey

Cave Moon Press
P.O. Box 1773, Yakima, WA 98907
ISBN-978-0-6925831-9-7
2017, paper, 86 pp., $12.95

Reviewed by Corrina Wycoff

Rules for Walking Out—Crysta Casey's second posthumously released poetry collection—chronicles Casey's life during and after military service. Her poems stretch from the Parris Island boot camp where her enlistment began in 1978, to the Seattle Veteran's Hospital where her life ended thirty years later. She rarely editorializes. Instead, with journalistic distance, Casey juxtaposes her experiences, revealing their complexity, and creating a deeply authentic, poignant memoir in verse.

An enlisted woman in the 1970s, Casey lived the sexual politics of Marine culture. A boot camp poem quotes the chaplain, who derides the all-female troop as "lesbians [and] whores" while the drill instructor asks, "How many of you joined because love is a pain in the ass?" This ambiguity between exploitation and agency recurs in several poems written about her time in active duty. In one, Casey's "legs [are] spread open to officers who . . . ask [her] to suck / them like a cherry popsicle, only hot / like corn on the cob." In another, she confesses, "I needed the money. They tipped well. I only knew them as fellow Marines; I had my own male friend off-base."

Casey serves under Captain Bowman. It is Bowman, ultimately, whose false allegations of Casey's suicide attempts result in her commitment to the military hospital's psychiatric ward. His authority as a male officer means more than the inaccuracies of his accusations. The volume's preface, "A Curse—for Captain Bowman," explains: "You told them I was slitting / my wrists . . . . You said, 'In the bathroom / in her room . . .' The toilets were down the hall. / You didn't even know / how enlisted people lived . . ."

While his mendacity seems clear, Bowman's sanity does not. Casey and other female lance corporals clean his office. One poem describes discarding plastic spoons they find in "coffee cups, where dried noodles / claw the sides like ivy," only to be shouted at, via intercom, "Where are my spoons?" Bowman "orders a detachment . . . to find some spoons." A prolonged scavenger hunt ensues for replacement spoons of the specific weight and thickness Bowman requires. Not long afterward, still on base but threatened with commitment to the psych ward, Casey aptly claims, "I am on the psych ward . . . The truth is, I am."

Once literally institutionalized, Casey receives a schizo-affective disorder diagnosis and begins "writing furiously in a new notebook" about the fellow soldiers she meets on the ward. Like Casey herself, they seem no more insane than the uninstitutionalized Captain Bowman. Anne, a fellow Marine, refuses to take the prescribed medicine. Casey writes, "I already swallowed mine. / Anne is sure I'll die." And Anne's worry isn't wholly wrong. Casey writes that her "thoughts are more exciting when [she's] not on meds." The meds trample and circumscribe her imagination. "On medication," she writes, "I think of vacuuming the carpet."

Casey relocates to Seattle in the 1980s after her honorable medical discharge. She is an indigent military veteran struggling with mental illness, yet poems about these post-military years remain keen and clear-eyed. One wryly describes Jim, the homebound, depressed Vietnam Vet who one day decides "to go downtown to the VA Regional Office and make sure he was going to get an American flag on his coffin," only to be told, by the clerk, that military records already list him as dead. Another observes a five-year-old boy playing by a fountain, pretending to have been shot in the head.

She writes of a Marine killed in Iraq and of a middle class civilian woman who, when asked why a nearby flag flies at half-mast, suggests Orville Redenbacher's death. She writes of her friend Kim, a cross-dresser and former bomber pilot, living in shoddy transient housing, directly across the street from the municipal campus where the courthouse stands.

Casey, also a self-taught painter, overlays these baldly rendered situations with deliberately colored images. One of her active duty poems mentions a visit she makes to her family during a Christmas leave. There, she receives a gift of acrylic paints: "red, yellow, blue, black, and white," all the colors needed to replicate the American flag and the Marines logo. Casey employs this palette as a central motif. On the psychiatric ward of the military hospital, she writes of living among "black sheep, white artists and poets." There, she will sit in the dayroom and "stack white, / blue, and red poker chips / into a tower, knock it down with dice, then pile the chips again." She writes of a Black female Marine found murdered in the barracks.

Sometimes, she mixes pigments. Writing of a literal self-portrait, she describes: "I wear a camouflage shirt . . . Only black nylons cover my legs . . . My feet are partially covered by black, open-toed high heels." She writes of the "green cammie shirt" she buys at a garage sale when, as a veteran, she finally declares herself "Private / General of [her] own Army." Finally, at the VA hospital, in yet another dayroom, she will "refuse to paint green or gold" on the paint-by-numbers set. She paints another self-portrait instead: "pink cheeks, red lips." She paints a hand below the portrait, paints numbers on its fingernails, "each with purple hues."

Describing her expression in this self-portrait, Casey deems it "sad as a baby's hunger." But a baby's hunger cannot always be assuaged by bottle or breast. The keening continues without protecting the listener's comfort, without assigning any blame, and without offering any advice. *Rules for Walking Out* is just as unapologetic, as innocent, and as discomfiting.

LOVE'S
LAST
NUMBER
POEMS
CHRISTOPHER HOWELL

Love's Last Number

by Christopher Howell
Milkweed Editions
https://milkweed.org/book/loves-last-number
ISBN-978-1-57131-475-8
2017, paper, 130 pp., $16.00

Reviewed by Polly Buckingham

Love's Last Number is a stunning, all encompassing collection, shiny and sad, wise and generous: think owls, King Arthur, and Mahler in a clef-shaped canoe.

We are invited from the first poem into the "song of our consciousness / that faltering old man," down a spring path and across a bridge, to this conclusion: "the old man listens for the one spot of silence / or the one clear voice that might be his own." The poem introduces oppositional forces that rely on one another to exist. It describes "memory's little ways and sudden corner-like loveliness / turned to smoke and broken glass it eats and eats / to stay marginally alive." The book, too, is not afraid to go to those places of glass eating and marginal survival, as the second section, a meditation on war, does in its examination of Howell's own military experiences, military history, and the mythology of war. Young men return broken; boy scouts participate in activities that will make them shameful later; and the Angel of Mars describes himself as a "gift no one will live to see."

Throughout the book, clarity and fog, as in the first poem, are played against one another; phrases like "cloudy light" appear repeatedly. Imagery of fog and glass place us again on a journey through both the real and imagined worlds, through the worlds of the narrator's childhood and young adulthood where love is beautiful, painful, and transitory, and "dreaming makes one stupid," through history, and through an imagined mythology where Tolstoy is a virtuous bartender and children are "catching faces in dip nets," faces that are "dreaming / of glass bones."

The angels and God and Jesus are all at times dismayed with us and other times equally as ambivalent and confused, moving forward down some mystical path or road or across a shining bridge. The cloudiness and ambiguity in the search for clarity appear on a cosmic level in the final lines of a couple poems: "God / bent as though happy / or blind" and "God's / emptiness or God's hopeful / and faraway gleam." But then, if the poet did not believe clarity could be had, even if only in "one spot of silence," what would be the point of all this musing? All this beauty in the face of darkness? All these forays into the unseen world, alive with crows who believe they are owls? After all, Howell writes, "all destinations turn to paths."

X

Raven Notes

metal green sand shovel, dip pen & India ink on paper, by Clare Johnson

LIST OF ARTISTS AND ILLUSTRATORS

Pages art/illustrations appear on:

NOTES, PERMISSIONS AND PUBLICATION CREDITS

Paul Hunter: "The Moment Was Dreamlike, Upsetting" was originally published in *Clownery*, by Paul Hunter, Davila Art & Books, Sisters, Oregon, 2017. Reprinted by permission of the author.

Marjorie Maddox: "Homecoming" was previously published in the literary journal *The Same*, and in *Local News from Someplace Else*, by Marjorie Maddox, Wipf and Stock, 2013. Reprinted by permission of the author.

BIOGRAPHICAL NOTES
ARTISTS/ILLUSTRATORS

David Anderson is an artist and historian from Omaha, Nebraska. He dwells in a brick house that was built in 1926. He lives with his best friend, and five little people. The five do not pay rent, but they do provide laughter. He enjoys swimming, writing, baseball, and playing chess. The photographs in this issue were inspired by experiencing winter in Omaha, and the feeling that there can be a profound element of joy that can exist with sadness and the past.

Nyri A. Bakkalian is a queer Armenian-American, and adopted Pittsburgher. She is an artist, writer, and historian whose work has appeared in *Inatri, Gutsy Broads*, and *QueerPGH*. She has a soft spot for local history and unknown stories, preferably uncovered during road trips. For more information, visit her blog at http://www.sparrowdreams.com or come say hello on Twitter at @riversidewings.

"The notion of 'home' can often be elusive and even fleeting. Some of us search our entire lives for home, while others leave behind the places they once called home. Here (*Riverside Home*, pg 80) the chimney of a ruined riverside home evokes home fires of long ago, and stands sentinel in a deep and peaceful forest. As I stood on mossy stones overlooking the coursing river, there was something melancholy but hopeful about the ruins. After all, home changes, but stories—be they the stories of former occupants or the stories of travelers visiting a darkened chimney—live forever."

Maria de Los Angeles is a New York City-based artist, raised in California, Mexican born. Her imagery focuses on issues of illegal migration, displacement, identity, and otherness, primarily using drawing, painting, installation, performance, fashion, and sculpture. De Los Angeles received her MFA in Painting and Printmaking from Yale University School of Art (2015), BFA in Fine Arts Painting from Pratt Institute (2013), and an Associate Degree in Fine Arts from Santa Rosa Junior College in Northern California.

Maria was recognized for her community-oriented projects such as the creation of art programs for youth. She received a Community Action Partnership's Award and the Blair Dickinson Memorial Prize from Yale University. She is a visiting Professor at Pratt Institute, and was an artist in residency at El Museo del Barrio (2017), and at Mana Contemporary (2015-2017). She is currently at work on a poetry collection and a series of tiny mutant essays about convertibles, lice, beekeeper's hats, and love.

Gabe Hales is a seventeen-year-old high schooler based out of Okemos, Michigan, who loves creating art with a camera lens. She works with major corporate companies, such as Context Summits, on photographic and videographic projects. She also does freelance work on the side for local businesses, bands, and events. Contact her at www.gabehales.weebly.com.

Streets of Chicago (pg 48): "I took two pieces of art that I captured in Chicago and merged them together in Photoshop. It was a simple process that only took a few minutes but created a fantastic result." *Seeing Shapes* (pg 51): "I was walking through a building in Chicago and decided to take some pictures, so I pulled out my iPhone to snap a shot and was rewarded with the beautiful contrast of black and white shadows that make up this image."

Clare Johnson (featured artist): "I'm often inspired by ordinary objects like band aids, which equally signify a wound and healing attention. My drawings, similarly, come from a sense of unease or worry—but are also how I soothe it. The act of drawing is comforting, lets me bring something into being, or spend time in a place that I also know can't quite exist in reality. For me, the pieces end up homesick—something is slightly out of reach. Many show scenes I have imagined since childhood—invented places or scenarios that provided me with a feeling of security when I struggled with asthma, insomnia, everyday worries about finances and relationships, loss of loved ones, homesickness during years of displacement. Through them I can make ordinary objects like mailboxes, houseplants, and laundry mysterious and magical, like secret gifts left by an invisible friend. The titles connect the world of the drawing to my actual world while making it, recording something I was thinking about as I finished each piece.

"I draw freehand using metal pen nibs dipped in India ink, with no pencil underdrawing or erasing. Once I start a drawing, I never discard it; if surprises happen I figure out how to incorporate them or change direction." Contact her via www.clarejohnson.com.

Srilatha Malladi: "Painting is Passion. My mother taught me painting in my childhood in Hyderabad, India. Later I learned it in school. I always use acrylic and oil colours on canvas for my paintings. I paint contemporary art work from different subjects, like landscapes, portraits, and still lifes."

Malladi's Solo Art Exhibitions in 2017: the ICCR Art Gallery, Hyderabad, Telangaana State, India, and in Bangalore, Karnataka State, India.

Michael C. Paul was born in Missouri, and studied history and political science at the University of Kansas, and the University of Miami. His short stories and illustrations have appeared in *The Door, Satire,* and *My Friend,* among other publications. He traipsed around a bit, both here and abroad, before settling down in Northern Virginia.

Jenn Powers is a writer and photographer who lives in New England. She is currently writing a memoir, and her most recent work is published or forthcoming in *Hayden's Ferry Review, Driftwood Press, Don't Talk to Me About Love,* and *Jet*

Fuel Review. Visit her at www.jennpowers.com. and follow her at Jenn @livinglife1107.

"There's beauty in simplicity. The photos *Tea II* (pg 56) and *Late Afternoon Light* (pg 170) were taken in my parents' home in Connecticut. It is also my childhood home, and it's the simple familiar details which evoke a sense of nostalgia: stacked teacups, squares of sunlight thrown across the floor, a vase of lilacs from the backyard, crystal, dark wood. It's the details that make up a life—and a home. Sometimes, the most beautiful things are the simplest—things that have been there all along—and I wanted to capture the feeling of home, my home, before time progresses to the point where that's no longer possible."

Rebecca Pyle (cover artist) began as an artist by drawing horses in sand. She is now an oil painter. Images of her oil paintings accompany others' stories and poems selected for *Hawai'i Review, New England Review, Inklette,* and, now, *Raven Chronicles.* She gardens a hundred-foot-long rock garden below her hundred-year-old gray brick house in the foothills of Salt Lake City, Utah. She is also a writer. Visit her art website: rebeccapyleartist.com.

Notes on the cover art:

"*The Fireplace in the Violinists' House* is drawn from a memory of a real fireplace, the fireplace in the home my youngest son, and many other violin students, receive weekly lessons in. The violinists' house I have painted is room-after-room bathed in shades of yellow, what I like to think of as an orchard yellow. Not because it suggests yellow apple or yellow pear or lemons. Because the yellow has a suggestion of that dullest and softest and most muted of greens, the green underside of an apple leaf. Or—because there is always something green and growing near the fireplace—sometimes a tree in a large pot, or, as in this painting, a cluster of branches not yet pulsed into bud. *A fireplace is an altar,* said Frank Lloyd Wright. This fireplace is one. It has levels of shape and whiteness, and it has a feeling as all fireplaces do of being ancient and being very new, too. The scroll-like shapes within the fireplace suggest the curled scrolls of violins, or the repeating, rising sounds of fire burning wood. In an Anderson fairy tale, logs in the fireplace and the wooden violins might have a sad bright conversation about the difference, and the similarity, of their fates. Above, I have painted strange swirls in the yellow wall above the fireplace, similar to the strange swirls in the fireplace. The cream-colored roses at left of mantel are very simple circular shapes—almost like the rounded shapes in notes, periods, or commas. The arching mirror above suggests imminent visitors or dwellers. If it was lower, it would have in it a great black piano across the room, a small round clock, and a framed image of a bird."

Robert Ransom is an artist who lives within the Snake River Plain of south central Idaho—a state he credits as being an artistic influence by virtue of its beauty, and a local culture that has had the effect of compressing subjectivity through the point of a ballpoint pen. For nearly thirty years he has begun each day with an hour working on an image corresponding to a repressed reality. An image may take between nine months and two years to complete, at which time he turns the page and begins again on the reverse image with the opposite hand.

Inye Wokoma completed a degree in journalism and filmmaking from Clark Atlanta University, Georgia, before establishing Ijo Arts Media Group in Seattle. His work for corporate and non-profit clients has appeared in *USA Today, ColorsNW, Washington Law and Politics*, and *Chicago Wilderness*, among others. Wokoma received a Telly Award in 2012; he has also received honors at the Colorado Environmental Film Festival, the Society of Professional Journalists Western Washington Chapter, and the National Council on Crime and Delinquency. His current exhibit at the Northwest African

American Museum, *An Elegant Utility,* explores the creation of place, identity, and the Northwest African American community that has historically characterized Seattle's Central District neighborhood.

Saint James Harris Wood was on the road with his psychedelic punk blues band, The Saint James Catastrophe, when he picked up the heroin-smoking habit. This inevitably led to a California high desert penal colony where he reinvented himself as a writer of the darkly absurd. His poetry, fiction, and essays have been published in *Confrontation, Meridian, Tears In The Fence, On Spec, Lynx Eye, The Sun,* and other less reputable literary gazettes.

Bill Yake has been taking photos of critters since high school and those early years ('65, '66) working in Glacier National Park in Montana. His first degree was in Zoology, and Ravens, with their handsome certainty and totemic linage, have always held a special allure. "This proud fellow (pg 39) was prowling the roadside at Bow Lake in Banff National Park, Alberta, Canada, and deigned to have his image captured. I'm grateful."

BIOGRAPHICAL NOTES
Writers

Luther Allen writes poems and designs buildings from Sumas Mountain, Washington. He facilitates SpeakEasy, a community poetry reading series in Bellingham, and is co-editor of *Noisy Water*, a poetry anthology featuring 101 Whatcom County poets. His collection of poems, *The View from Lummi Island*, can be found at http://othermindpress.wordpress.com. His work is included in *WA 129*, an anthology of poems from Washington poets, edited by Tod Marshall, 2016-2018 Washington State Poet Laureate.

Dianne Aprile teaches on the faculty of Spalding University's low-residency MFA in Writing program. A former journalist and jazz club owner, she's published poems and four nonfiction books, edited prose and poetry volumes, and collaborated with visual artists on literary and gallery projects. She and her husband live in Kirkland, where she's completing a hybrid memoir, two sections of which received Pushcart nominations. As a staff writer for *The Courier-Journal*, out of Louisville, Kentucky, she was part of a team that won a Pulitzer Prize.

Anna Bálint edited *Words from the Café*, an anthology of writing from people in recovery. She is also the author of *Horse Thief*, a collection of short fiction spanning cultures and continents, and two earlier books of poetry. Her poems, stories, and essays have appeared in numerous journals and magazines, recently in *Riverbabble* and *Sparrow Trill, Minerva Rising's* special issue on race in America. Anna is an alumna of Hedgebrook Writers Retreat, the Jack Straw Writers Program, and has received awards/grants from the Seattle Arts Commission and 4Culture. In 2001, she received a Leading Voice Award in recognition of her creative work with urban youth at El Centro de la Raza. She has taught creative writing for many years and in many places, including in prisons, El Centro de la Raza, Antioch University, and Richard Hugo House. Currently, she teaches adults in recovery from the traumas of homelessness, addiction, and mental illness. She is a teaching artist with Seattle's Path With Art, and the founder of Safe Place Writing Circle at Recovery Café in Seattle.

Virginia Barrett's work has most recently appeared in *Poetry of Resistance: A Multicultural Anthology in Response to Arizona SB 1070* (University of Arizona Press), *New Mexico Review, Midnight Circus, Belle Reve,* and *Apple Valley Review*. Her chapbook, *Stars By Any Other Name,* was a semi-finalist for the 2017 Frost Place Chapbook Competition sponsored by Bull City Press. She is the recipient of a 2017 writer's residency grant from the Helene Wurlitzer Foundation. Virginia lives in San Francisco, where she is a writer, educator, editor, and activist.

Maria Batayola is co-founder of TEA, the forerunner of Northwest Asian American Theatre. She is a produced playwright, journalist, and poet, now working on her memoirs. Batayola has been straddling cultures since her parents brought her to Seattle from the Philippines as a teenager. So logically her writing themes are about recreating home, joy, connections, and social justice. She co-chairs the nine-year-old Pinoy Words Expressed Kultura Arts, organized to "promote Filipino American arts, culture, and heritage."

Michele Bombardier is a Northwest poet whose work has appeared in *Bellevue Literary Review, Fourth River, Artemis, Sukoon, The Examined Life Journal, Floating Bridge Review,* and others. She is completing her MFA in Poetry at Pacific University in Portland, Oregon, and works as a speech-language pathologist with persons with stroke, head injury, and autism.

Polly Buckingham's collection, *The Expense of a View,* won the Katherine Anne Porter Prize in Short Fiction (2016). Her chapbook, *A Year of Silence,* won the Jeanne Leiby Memorial Chapbook Award (2014), and she was the recipient of a 2014 Washington State Artists Trust fellowship. Her work appears in *The Gettysburg Review, The Threepenny Review* (reprinted at poetrydaily.com), *Hanging Loose, Witness, North American Review, The Poetry Review,* and elsewhere. Polly is founding editor of StringTown Press. She teaches creative writing at Eastern Washington University, and is Associate Director of Willow Springs Books.

Elizabeth Burnam grew up in a yellow trailer in Jamesville, New York, keeping secrets and getting her feet dirty. Now she lives in Burlington, Vermont, where she is enrolled in Champlain College's program in Professional Writing.

Jim Cantú has penned poems, prose, and personal essays. He was one of the 2016 Port Townsend, Washington "Angels of History" presenters, and read flash fiction at the 2016 Seattle Lit Crawl. In August, 2016, he was the "Writer-In-Residence" for the month-long "La Cocina," a Pop-Up Latinx Artists' Salon hosted by La Sala, held in conjunction with the Seattle Art Fair. His poem "Birthday" appeared in the February, 2016 issue of online *Whirlwind Magazine.* In 2015, his poem "Where is My Home?" was included in 4Culture's/King County Metro's "Poetry on the Buses" project. He is a graduate of the Artist Trust 2016 Edge for Literary Artists program.

Jennifer Clark is the author of *Necessary Clearings* (Shabda Press, 2014). This collection of grief and loss poems was nominated for a Michigan Notable book, and made the Kalamazoo Public Library Staff Picks: Best of 2014. Her second poetry collection, *Johnny Appleseed: The Slice and Times of John Chapman,* is forthcoming from Shabda Press. A former contributor to *Raven Chronicles,* her work has also appeared in *Flyway, Nimrod, Concho River Review, Columbia Journal* and *Ecotone.* She lives in Kalamazoo, Michigan, not far from Creston Street.

Cheryce (Chy) Clayton is not a cat. She is a writer; however, she was not there and did not eat the whole thing. You will not find her here today, but at amazon.com/author/cheryceclayton, where she writes cyberpunked space opera, sf, horror, and zombie pron. She is Choctaw, Two Spirit, [etc.]. Please stop reading now and check out her contributions.

T. Clear is a founder of Floating Bridge Press and Easy Speak Seattle, a twice-monthly open mic venue. Her work has appeared in many magazines, including *Cascadia Review, Crab Creek Review, Poetry Northwest, The Moth,* and *Atlanta Review*. Her work has been nominated for Independent Best American Poetry, and a Pushcart Prize.

Minnie A. Collins, author of *The Purple Wash* (2013), is published in *Emerald Reflections, Threads, Crosscurrents, Quiet Shorts, Washington English Journal,* and *Innovation Abstracts* at the University of Texas at Austin. Among her awards are Seattle University's Administrator of the Year and African American Alumni Achievement, Dan Evans Innovation Award, National Institute for Staff and Organizational Development (NISOD) Teaching Excellence from the University of Texas at Austin, and Who's Who Among American Teachers.

Mary Eliza Crane is a native of New England who migrated to the Pacific Northwest three decades ago and settled into the Cascade foothills east of Puget Sound. A regular feature at poetry venues throughout the Puget Sound region, she has read her poetry from Woodstock to Los Angeles. Mary has two volumes of poetry, *What I Can Hold In My Hands* (Gazoobi Tales Publishing, 2009), and *At First Light* (Gazoobi Tales Publishing, 2011). Her work has appeared in *Raven Chronicles, The Cartier Street Review, Tuesday Poems, Quill and Parchment, The Far Field, Avocet,* and several anthologies, including *The LitFUSE Anthology*, and *WA 129*, an anthology of poems from Washington poets, edited by Tod Marshall,

2016-2018 Washington State Poet Laureate.

Larry Crist lives in Humboldt County, Northern California, and has one poetry collection: *Undertow Overtures*, ATOM Press, available through Amazon. He misses Seattle immensely, where he lived for the past twenty-five years.

Jenny L. Davis is a citizen of the Chickasaw Nation, and originally from Oklahoma. She is an assistant professor at the University of Illinois at Urbana-Champaign, where she lives with her partner and spends most of her time tending her cats (and cat-sized Chihuahua), plants, and the students in her American Indian Studies and Anthropology classes. Both her research and activism center on contemporary indigenous identity, indigenous language revitalization, and the Two-Spirit community.

Risa Denenberg lives in Sequim, Washington, where she works as a nurse practitioner. She is an editor at Headmistress Press, an independent publisher of poetry by lesbians. She has published three chapbooks, and two full-length books of poetry, most recently, *Whirlwind @ Lesbos* (Headmistress Press, 2016). Her collection, *A Slight Faith*, is forthcoming in 2018, from MoonPath Press.

Patrick Dixon is a retired teacher and commercial fisherman who has been published in *Oregon Coast, The Journal of Family Life, National Fisherman, Oberon, FISH,* and other publications. He is the editor of the seven-book anthology of fisherpoetry, *Anchored in Deep Water* (2014). His chapbook, *Arc of Visibility*, won the 2015 Alabama State Poetry Society's annual Morris Memorial competition.

Larry Eickstaedt is an Iowa farm boy who became a marine biologist. He was a founding faculty member at The Evergreen State College in Olympia, Washington, and he writes poetry and sculpts stone. His poems have appeared in *Minotaur, Heartland Outdoors,* and *Spitball.* He lives in Olympia, where he recently constructed an artistic tree house.

Anita Endrezze, poet and artist, continues to move between the almost impassable wall of MS and the freedom of a world open to art and multicultural ideas. She was inspired to write her poem "The Wall" (pg 22) to protest in a literal and symbolic way. Her grandmother came from Mexico a hundred years ago. A recent altered-book project will be archived in the Smithsonian. She also writes fiction and poetry. Her latest collection of poems and art appear in the chapbook, *A Thousand Branches,* by Red Bird Press.

Diane Glancy is professor emerita at Macalester College in St. Paul, Minnesota. In 2017, she published: *QWERTYUIOPASDFGHJKLZXCVBNM* (*The Keyboard Letters*) (poetry); *Mary Queen of Bees,* a novella about Mary Wesley, sister of John Wesley, who founded the Methodist Church; and *The Servitude of Love* (short stories). In 2016, *The Collector of Bodies: Concern for Syria and the Middle East* (poetry), was published by Wipf and Stock. In 2015, *Report to the Department of the Interior: Poems,* won the Willa Award from Women Writers of the West. She edited, along with Linda Rodriguez, *The World Is One Place, Native American Poets Visit the Middle East,* University of Missouri, Kansas City, 2017.

Penny Harter's recent books include *The Resonance Around Us* (2013); *One Bowl* (2012); and *Recycling Starlight* (2010; reprint 2017). Recent work has appeared, or is forthcoming, in a number of journals, including *Adanna, Persimmon Tree, Rattle, Tiferet,* and *Tattoo Highway,* as well as in numerous anthologies. A featured reader at both the first (1985) and the 2010 Dodge Poetry Festivals, she has won three fellowships from the New Jersey State Council on the Arts; the Mary Carolyn Davies Award from the Poetry Society of America; and two residencies from the Virginia Center for the Creative Arts (January, 2011, and March, 2015). She lives in the southern New Jersey shore area.

Sharon Hashimoto teaches at Highline College in Des Moines, Washington. Her book of poetry, *The Crane Wife,* was co-winner of the Nicholas Roerich Prize and published by Story Line Press in 2003. She is a recipient of a National Endowment for the Arts fellowship in poetry. Her stories and poetry have appeared in *North American Review, Crab Orchard Review, Bamboo Ridge, Tampa Review, Shenandoah, River Styx, Raven Chronicles,* and many other literary publications. She is currently working on a novel.

Thomas Hubbard, a retired writing instructor and spoken word performer, authored *Nail and other hardworking poems,* Year of the Dragon Press, 1994; *Junkyard Dogz* (also available on audio CD); and *Injunz,* a chapbook. He designed and published *Children Remember Their Fathers* (an anthology), and books by seven other authors. His book reviews have appeared in *Square Lake, Raven Chronicles, New Pages* and *The Cartier Street Review.* Recent publication credits include poems in *Yellow Medicine Review, I Was Indian,* editor Susan Deer Cloud, *Florida Review,* and short stories in *Red Ink* and *Yellow Medicine Review.* He serves editorially with *Raven Chronicles* and *The Cartier Street Review,* and he still performs spoken word occasionally in and around Seattle, and at various other venues around the country.

Tom C. Hunley is a professor of English and Creative Writing at Western Kentucky University. His work has appeared in many literary periodicals, such as *TriQuarterly, Five Points, North American Review,* and *New York Quarterly.* With Alexandria Peary, he co-edited *Creative Writing Pedagogies for the Twenty-First Century* (Southern Illinois State University Press, 2015). His poems in this issue of *Raven Chronicles* are from his sixth full-length collection, *Here Lies*, forthcoming in 2018 from Stephen Foster Austin State University Press.

Clare Johnson is a writer and artist, originally from Seattle. She is a Michael S. Harper Poetry Prize winner, and a Hugo House New Works Competition finalist. Publication credits include *Blithe House Quarterly, quiet Shorts, Cranky, Jack Straw Anthology, Poetry Northwest*, and *Shake The Tree*. Solo exhibitions include Oxford's North Wall, Bridport Arts Centre, Hugo House, Storefronts Seattle, and London's Guy's Hospital. Her Post-it Note Project won a *Seattle Magazine Best of 2011* for "Best New Take on the Memoir" and a cover feature in *Real Change News*. In recent years, Johnson received Artist Trust funding to expand her series of drawings inspired by favorite books, published *Roses* (a book pairing her art with Rilke poetry), and was a Jack Straw Writing Fellow. She also designed interactive digital backdrops (funded in part by 4Culture) for a 2017 East Coast production of *Our Town*, combining drawings, painting, and erasure poems written from Thornton Wilder's script. See more of her visual and written work at www.clarejohnson.com.

Sarah Jones is a poet and freelance writer who lives in Seattle. She is on the staff of *Poetry Northwest*, and her work has appeared in *Entropy, The Normal School, City Arts Magazine, Yes, Poetry*, and other publications.

J.I. Kleinberg is a Pushcart Prize nominee and winner of the 2016 Ken Warfel Fellowship. She is co-editor of *Noisy Water: Poetry from Whatcom County, Washington* (Other Mind Press, 2015). Her poetry has appeared recently in *One, Diagram, Otoliths, Poetry Breakfast*, and elsewhere. She lives in Bellingham, Washington, and blogs most days at chocolateisaverb.wordpress.com and thepoetrydepartment.wordpress.com.

Martha Kreiner works as a registered nurse with Healthcare for the Homeless in Seattle. She holds an MA in Creative Writing from Michigan State University, and her work has appeared in *Seattle Review of Books, Windfall, Floating Bridge Review, ILK journal*, and *Hubbub*. She was a Jack Straw Writer in 2015, when her poem "He Wanted to Die Anywhere But the Street" was featured on KUOW. With her beloved partner Amy, she is drafting a dystopian tween novella they hope to publish one day, under a name no one will recognize.

Gina B. LaLonde was born and raised in Seattle. Her fiction, poems, and screenplays reflect the unique identity and grit of the Emerald City and its people. She was the recipient of the Michener Fellowship from 2014-2016 in Austin, Texas. In winter, 2016, her screenplay won the title of semi-finalist in the Seattle International Film Festival Catalyst Screenplay Competition. She graduated with honors and was awarded the WTC Johnson Fellowship from New York University film school; her work was recognized as a Sundance Institute finalist; she's been honored with the Future Filmmaker Award from Women in Film Seattle; she earned a top-five Honorable Mention from the International Screenwriters' Association's Fast Track Mentorship Program. She's now in the process of completing a book of fiction, titled "The Hazard of Talking to Ghosts," while continuing to write screenplays and poetry.

Charles Leggett is a professional actor based in Seattle, Washington. His poetry has been published locally in *The Raven Chronicles, Volume 20, Soundtracks, Floating Bridge Review, Barnwood International Poetry Magazine, The Far Field, Clover: A Literary Rag,* and *FRIGG: A Magazine of Fiction and Poetry*; in over three dozen journals throughout the U.S., the UK, Ireland, Australia, New Zealand, and Canada. He has twice been nominated for the Pushcart Prize. His long poem *Premature Tombeau for John Ashbery* was an e-chapbook in Barnwood Press's "Great Find" series.

Joan McBride is a Washington State representative and former mayor of Kirkland, Washington. She enjoys the intrinsic tension between poetry and politics. Recently she was published in *Clamor Magazine.*

Tanya McDonald is known for her love of chickens, haiku, and tea. A resident of Woodinville, Washington, she is easily identified by her brightly-colored plumage. Her poetry has appeared in various haiku journals, and she is currently serving as the vice president of Haiku Northwest.

Marjorie Maddox is Sage Graduate Fellow of Cornell University (MFA), and Professor of English and Creative Writing at Lock Haven University. She has published eleven collections of poetry—including *True, False, None of the Above* (Poiema Poetry Series and Illumination Book Award medalist); *Local News from Someplace Else*; *Wives' Tales*; *Transplant, Transport, Transubstantiation* (Yellowglen Prize); and *Perpendicular As I* (Sandstone Book Award); and over 500 stories, essays, and poems in journals and anthologies. Co-editor of *Common Wealth: Contemporary Poets on Pennsylvania* (Penn State Press), she also has published four children's books. For more information, visit www.marjoriemaddox.com.

Maiah Alicia Merino, a Latina-Native writer, lives and works in Seattle in the field of health and healing—employing both indigenous and western forms of healing. She had two poems, in 2016 and 2017, featured in 4Culture's Poetry On Buses Project. She had two poems published in *Revolution and Reclamation,* Art Night Books, 2014. The essay, "Walls and Bridges" (pg 24), highlights the writer's experiences of walls and bridges, both physical and metaphorical, that have helped her struggle with ideas of good and evil. Still an emerging writer, and mother of a four-year-old son, "the words surrender to the page after the prince greets the stars."

Kate Miller is a poet, writer, and teacher who lives in Bellingham, Washington, with her wife and dog. She teaches Gender Studies and American Cultural Studies at Western Washington University, and is working on a memoir. She has been published in several local anthologies and *Cirque Magazine,* and loves her Bellingham writers' community.

Kevin Miller lives in Tacoma, Washington. Recent poems have appeared in *Clover, Terrain.org, Cirque,* and *Spitball.* Miller was a teacher for forty years, and now drives the progeny bus.

Elizabeth Myhr is a poet, editor, and publisher. She holds a BA from The Evergreen State College and an MFA from Seattle Pacific University. She served as an artist-in-residence at Centrum in Port Townsend, Washington, and is a Milotte Foundation scholar for her work promoting nature poetry devoted to the health of the earth. In 2010, Myhr co-founded Calypso Editions, a virtual, cooperative press that specializes in literature in translation and emerging writers. Her poetry has appeared in *Alaska Quarterly Review, Poetry International, elephant journal,* and other publications. Elizabeth Myhr lives and works in Seattle.

Shankar Narayan explores identity, power, and race in a world where the body is flung across borders yet possesses unrivaled power to transcend them. A Pushcart Prize nominee, a 2016 Fellow at Kundiman and Richard Hugo House, and the winner of the 2017 Iowa Sweet Corn Prize in Poetry, Shankar draws strength from his global upbringing and from his work as a civil rights attorney. His work appears in *Jaggery, Panoply, Crab Creek Review, Raven Chronicles, The Litfuse Anthology,* and *WA 129,* an anthology of poems edited by Tod Marshall, 2016-2018 Washington State Poet Laureate. In Seattle, he awakens to the wonders of Cascadia every day, but his heart yearns east to his other hometown, Delhi.

Soonest Iheanyi Nathaniel is a journalist, teacher, poet, and spokenword artist. He lives in Lagos, Nigeria, where he was born. He has a degree in Mathematics and Computer Science. His poems have been published in *Pedestal Magazine, Erbacce Poetry Journal* (UK), *Elsewhere Lit, ANA Review, Praxis Lit, Saraba Mag, Sentinel Nigeria, Kalahari Review, Loudthotz Poetry, Asa Planet, Blue Lotus Muse,* among others. He won the You Poetry Contest in 2015, Korea-Nigeria Poetry Prize in 2014, Futo Writers Award in 2011, and IFM Prize in 2010. In his spare time, you can find him listening to the music of the spheres, reading the stars, or trying to woo the moon.

Don Noel: Retired after four decades of prizewinning print and broadcast journalism in Hartford, Connecticut, Don received his MFA in Creative Writing from Fairfield University in 2013. His fiction has been published in numerous journals, including *Calliope, Shark Reef, Drunk Monkeys, The Tau, Indian River Review, Midnight Circus, Oracle, Clare Literary Magazine, The Raven's Perch, The Violet Hour, Literary Heist, Dime Show Review,* and *Yellow Chair Review*. He has a novel and two novellas that are still languishing.

John Olson is the author of numerous books of poetry and prose poetry, including *Echo Regime, Free Stream Velocity, Backscatter: New and Selected Poems, Larynx Galaxy,* and *Dada Budapest* (June, 2017). He was the recipient of *The Stranger's* 2004 Genius Award for Literature, and in 2012 was one of eight finalists for the Washington State Arts Innovator Award. He has also published four novels, including *Souls of Wind* (shortlisted for The Believer Book Award), *The Nothing That Is, The Seeing Machine,* and *In Advance of the Broken Justy*.

Sue Pace's poetry, short stories, nonfiction, and personal essays have appeared in over 120 publications. Her most recent collection, "Driving Sharon Crazy," contains fifteen related short stories and all but one have been previously published.

Her story in this issue of *Raven Chronicles,* "The Library Study" (pg 171) is part of a collection of ten related short stories. Pace worked for nineteen years as a field interviewer for a variety of nonprofits, including the CDC, the Department of Energy, DSHS, the Gallop Poll, and various universities. She "met a lot of heroes over the past two decades."

Linda Packard's poems have been published in *Crab Creek Review, Fine Madness, Matrix, Napa Review, Poetry Seattle,* and *Puget Soundings,* among other publications. Her poem "Aftershock" appears in the chapbook *Expression,* now available from Arts & Humanities Bainbridge, 2017. Linda facilitates various workshops through Seattle's The Vajra, including Writing as a Spiritual Practice and SoulCollage.

Michael Philips is an Egyptian-Canadian writer. He is the author of two novels, *Assiut Citystan* (2009), and *Sonquor's Crime* (2011). Michael lived in Cairo between 2010-2014, where he practiced medicine, took part in the Egyptian Revolution of 2011, and wrote fiction in Arabic. In 2014, he moved to Toronto, Canada, and began writing in English. His articles have been published by the NATO Council of Canada, where he was a research analyst between 2014-2016. Michael now works with children with intellectual disabilities, and lives in the city of Belleville, Ontario.

David J.S. Pickering is a native of the north Oregon coast and has lived in Oregon his entire life. His poetry has been published in *The Sunday Oregonian, Portland Review, Gertrude Journal,* and in the anthology *Salt: A Collection of Poetry on the Oregon Coast,* 2005. Because he earns his living as a human resources director, he made time to write on Saturdays in one of Portland's many coffee houses where he didn't quite fit in with the neighborhood hipsters and college students. He recently moved with his husband to The Dalles, a town sadly bereft of good coffee joints. He continues to write, anyway.

Susan Noyes Platt is the author of *Art and Politics Now: Cultural Activism in a Time of Crisis,* Midmarch Arts Press, 2011, and *Art and Politics in the 1930s: Modernism, Marxism, Americanism,* Midmarch Arts Press, 1999. She has a MA from Brown University, and a Ph.D. from the University of Texas at Austin. She is based in Seattle and her main interest is writing about art that engages social issues. She curated three exhibitions at the M. Rosetta Hunter Art Gallery at Seattle Central College: "The Global Art Coalition," "The Art of Selma Waldman," and "Cultural Activism in a Time of Crisis." She blogs at www.artandpoliticsnow.com.

Rebecca Francesca Reuter is currently a first-year MFA student in a low residency creative writing program at the Institute of American Indian Arts. "Finding the Girl from Guantanamo" (pg 205) is her first published piece. Writing is Rebecca's second love. Her first love was and still is marine biology. She holds a BA in Biology from University of Chicago, and a MA in Marine Science from California State University's Moss Landing Marine Laboratory. She currently works as a communications specialist at NOAA's Alaska Fisheries Science Center in Seattle, Washington. In her career as a nonfiction writer, Rebecca hopes to capitalize on her experiences as a first generation child born in the USA, as a person of mixed cultural heritage, and her childhood experiences in the inner-city of Chicago.

J. R. Robinson is a twenty-five-year-old Polish-born writer who lives in Charlotte, North Carolina, with her husband and two dogs. She has a BA in Chinese Literature and Asian Languages and a BBA in Finance from the University of Texas at Austin. She currently works at a Big 4 auditing firm as a finance consultant and spends a lot of time on the road advising clients all over the world. Due to her hectic work life, she does most of her writing at airports and in-between business meetings. In her spare time, she enjoys reading, playing tennis, video editing, and playing with her dogs.

Robert Ronnow's most recent poetry collections are *New & Selected Poems: 1975-2005* (Barnwood Press, 2007), and *Communicating the Bird* (Broken Publications, 2012). He lives in Williamstown, Massachusetts. Visit his website at www.ronnowpoetry.com.

Frank Rossini grew up in New York City, and moved to Eugene, Oregon, in 1972. He taught at the University of Oregon and Lane Community College for thirty-eight years. He has published work in various journals, including *The Seattle Review, Chiron Review, Clackamas Review, The Mas Tequila Review*, and *Paterson Literary Review*. Silverfish Review Press published a chapbook of his poems, *sparking the rain*, and sight | for | sight books, an offshoot of Silverfish Review Books, published his book of poems, *midnight the blues* (2012).

Terry Sanville lives in San Luis Obispo, California, with his artist-poet wife (his in-house editor) and one skittery cat (his in-house critic). He writes full-time, producing short stories, essays, poems, and novels. Since 2005, his short stories have been accepted by more than 250 literary and commercial journals, magazines, and anthologies, including *The Potomac Review, The Bitter Oleander, Shenandoah*, and *Conclave: A Journal of Character*. He was nominated twice for Pushcart Prizes, for his stories "The Sweeper" and "The Garage." Terry is a retired urban planner and an accomplished jazz and blues guitarist —who once played with a symphony orchestra backing up jazz legend George Shearing.

Judith Skillman's latest book is *Kafka's Shadow*, Deerbrook Editions, 2017. Her poems have appeared in *Poetry, FIELD, Tampa Review, The Southern Review, The Iowa Review, Midwest Quarterly Review, Seneca Review, Prairie Schooner, The Bloomsbury Anthology of Jewish American Poets*, and other journals and anthologies. She was a Writer in Residence at Centrum Foundation in Port Townsend, Washington, and at Hedgebrook Writers in Residence Program. At the Center for French Translation in Seneffe, Belgium, she translated Belgian-French poet Anne-Marie Derèse. A Jack Straw Foundation Writer in 2008 for poetry, and in 2013 for fiction, Skillman's poetry has been nominated for Pushcart Prizes. She received the UK Kit Award, Best of the Web, and her work is included in *Best Indie Verse of New England*. Awards include an Eric Mathieu King Fund grant from the Academy of American Poets. Visit her website at www.judithskillman.com.

Joannie Stangeland's poems have been published in *Ascent, Chiron Review, Cider Press Review, Cold Mountain Review, Crab Creek Review, Georgetown Review, Hubbub, Iodal, Melusine: Woman in the 21st Century, San Pedro River Review, Santa Fe Literary Review, The Comstock Review, Tulane Review*, and other journals. Books: *In Both Hands* (Ravenna Press, 2014), *Into the Rumored Spring* (Ravenna Press, 2011).Chapbooks: *A Piece of Work* (Ravenna Press, 2014), *A Steady Longing for Flight* (Floating Bridge Press, 1995), *Weathered Steps* (Rose Alley Press, 2002). Visit her website at joanniestangeland.com.

Alison Stone has published five poetry collections, including *Ordinary Magic* (New York Quarterly Books, 2016), *Dangerous Enough* (Presa Press, 2014), and *They Sing at Midnight*, which won the 2003 Many Mountains Moving Poetry Award. Her poems have appeared in *The Paris Review, Poetry, Ploughshares, Barrow Street, Poet Lore*, and many other journals and anthologies. She has been awarded Poetry Foundation's Frederick Bock Prize and New York Quarterly's Madeline Sadin award. She is also a painter and the creator of The Stone Tarot. A licensed psychotherapist, she has private practices in New York City and Nyack, New York. She is currently editing an anthology of poems on the Persephone/Demeter myth. Visit her at www.stonepoetry.org or www.stonetarot.com.

Mark Trechock is a native of Minneapolis, but lives in Dickinson, North Dakota, where he worked for many years as director of Dakota Resource Council, a rural community-organizing effort. He published his first poem in 1974. This year his poems have appeared in *Tipton Poetry Journal, Whimperbang, Triggerfish, High Desert Journal, Passager, Jonah Magazine,* and *Southern Pacific Review*. He likes to write about food, the Great Plains, and Latin America, where he has often traveled.

Angie Trudell Vasquez is a poet, writer, activist, and publisher. Her poetry, essays, and op-eds have appeared in print and on stage, nationally and internationally. Her poems have been published most recently in the *San Diego Annual Review* and in *Yellow Medicine Review*. She was a panelist at Split This Rock in Washington, D.C., in April, 2017. She is currently getting her MFA in poetry at IAIA, the Institute of American Indian Arts, in Santa Fe, New Mexico.

Michael Dylan Welch served two terms as poet laureate for Redmond, Washington, where he also curates two poetry reading series. His haiku and longer poetry have appeared in hundreds of journals and anthologies, including three Norton poetry anthologies, in at least twenty-two languages. Michael runs National Haiku Writing Month (www.nahaiwrimo.com), and is a founder and director of the biennial Haiku North America Conference. He co-founded the American Haiku Archives and founded the Tanka Society of America. His latest book is *Seven Suns/Seven Moons* (NeoPoiesis Press), co-written with Tanya McDonald. You can read about his books at www.graceguts.com, where he also posts many poems, essays, and reviews.

Diana Woodcock is the author of two full-length collections of poetry, most recently *Under the Spell of a Persian Nightingale*.

Her first collection, *Swaying on the Elephant's Shoulders*, won the 2010 Venice Quebodeaux International Women's Poetry Prize. Her third, *Tread Softly*, is forthcoming from Future-Cycle Press. Her seventh chapbook, *Near the Arctic Circle*, is forthcoming from Tiger's Eye Press. Since receiving an MFA degree in Creative Writing in 2004, she has been teaching creative writing, environmental literature and composition at Virginia Commonwealth University in Qatar. Previously, she spent nearly eight years working in Tibet, Macau, and on the Thai-Cambodian border. She is a Ph.D candidate (creative writing/poetry) at Lancaster University, UK.

Carolyne Wright co-edited the groundbreaking anthology, *Raising Lilly Ledbetter: Women Poets Occupy the Workspace* (Lost Horse Press, 2015), which received ten Pushcart Prize nominations and was a finalist in *Foreword Review's* Book of the Year Awards. She has nine poetry volumes, five books of poetry in translation, and a collection of essays. She received Fulbright, NEA, and Instituto Sacatar (Brazil) fellowships, among others. Her work has appeared before in *Raven Chronicles*, and she now serves on the Advisory Board. She teaches for Seattle's Richard Hugo House and the Antioch University Los Angeles MFA Program.

Corrina Wycoff is the author of two books of fiction, *O Street*, a novel-in-stories (OV Press, 2008), and *Damascus House*, a novel (Spuyten Duyvil, 2016). Her fiction and essays have also appeared in many journals and anthologies. She lives in Seattle and teaches English at Pierce College.

BIOGRAPHICAL NOTES
Editors

Kathleen Alcalá (Fiction Editor) is the author of a short story collection, three novels set in 19th century Mexico and the Southwest, and a collection of essays based on family history. Her work has received the Western States Book Award, the Governor's Writers Award, and a Pacific Northwest Booksellers Association Book Award. She received her second Artist Trust Fellowship in 2008, and was honored by the national Latino writers group, Con Tinta, at the Associated Writing Programs Conference in 2014. She has been designated an Island Treasure in the Arts. Kathleen's latest book is *The Deepest Roots: Finding Food and Community on a Pacific Northwest Island*, 2016, University of Washington Press.

Phoebe Bosché (Managing Editor) is a cultural activist, and has been managing editor of The Raven Chronicles literary organization / Raven Chronicles Press since 1991. She is a full-time editor and book designer. Her favorite poet is Archy, the cockroach, whose muse is Mehitabel, the alley cat.

Paul Hunter (Poetry Editor) has published fine letterpress poetry under the imprint of Wood Works Press since 1994: twenty-six books and over sixty broadsides. His poems have appeared in *Alaska Fisherman's Journal, Beloit Poetry Journal, Bloomsbury Review, Iowa Review, North American Review, Poetry, Poetry Northwest, Prairie Schooner, Raven Chronicles, The Small Farmer's Journal, The Southern Review, Spoon River Poetry Review* and *Windfall*, as well as in seven full-length books and three chapbooks. His first collection of farming poems, *Breaking Ground*, 2004, from Silverfish Review Press, was reviewed in *The New York Times*, and received the 2004 Washington State Book Award. A second volume of farming poems, *Ripening*, was published in 2007, a third companion volume, *Come the Harvest*, appeared in 2008, and the fourth from the same publisher, *Stubble Field*, appeared in 2012. He has been a featured poet on *The News Hour*, and has a prose book on small-scale, sustainable farming, *One Seed to Another: The New Small Farming*, published by the Small Farmer's Journal. His new book of prose poetry, *Clownery, In lieu of a life spent in harness*, was published in 2017 by Davila Art & Books, Sisters, Oregon.

Stephanie Lawyer (Nonfiction Editor) grew up in Mexico and has lived and worked in the U.S., the UK, and Asia. She edited in-house for Secker & Warburg in London, and Little, Brown in Boston, and worked for more than a decade in Hong Kong as a freelance editor and literary agent. Since moving to the West Coast in 1995, she has judged fiction for the Kiriyama Book Prize, edited the prize's online magazine, the *WaterBridge Review*, and worked with *Raven Chronicles* as an editor and a board member. Stephanie is currently an independent editor based in Seattle with an interest in literary fiction, nonfiction, and translation. She is developing an online project to promote new immigrant writers and emerging literary translators.

ACKNOWLEDGMENTS

Raven is indebted to our 2017 co-sponsors for partial funding of our programs: the Seattle Office of Arts & Culture (Civic Partners); 4Culture / King County Lodging Tax (Arts Sustained Support Program); the Washington State Arts Commission / ArtsWA, with National Endowment (NEA) funding; and all Raven subscribers and donors. Special thanks to Jack Straw Cultural Center, and Joan Rabinowitz, for office space and support of our reading series at the Jack Straw Studios in the University District, City of Seattle. And thanks to the generosity of three donors (**Larry Laurence**, **Alfredo Arrequin**, and **Kevin Miller**) for their generous donations in support of this Raven publication and our ongoing programs.

Founded in 1991
Vol. 24, Spring/Summer 2017
www.ravenchronicles.org

Publisher

Raven Chronicles Press,
501(c)(3) Organization

Subscriptions 2017
U.S.: $20/year (2 issues)
Single Issues: $11.99
Print & online support: $30/year
International: $24/year plus postage

All Queries
The Raven Chronicles
Mailing Address:
15528 12th Avenue NE
Shoreline, WA 98155
Street Address:
Jack Straw Cultural Center
Suite 205
909 NE 43rd St.
Seattle, WA 98105-6020

Tel: 206.941.2955
www.ravenchronicles.org
editors@ravenchronicles.org

Made in the USA
San Bernardino, CA
07 June 2017